Darwin, Carlyle,

AND

Dickens,

WITH OTHER ESSAYS.

Darwin, Carlyle,

AND

Dickens,

WITH OTHER ESSAYS.

BY

SAMUEL DAVEY, F.R.S.L., &c.

HASKELL HOUSE PUBLISHERS Ltd.
Publishers of Scarce Scholarly Books
NEW YORK, N. Y. 10012
1971

824.8
D248d

First Published 1876

HASKELL HOUSE PUBLISHERS LTD.
Publishers of Scarce Scholarly Books
280 LAFAYETTE STREET
NEW YORK, N. Y. 10012

Library of Congress Catalog Card Number: 77-116791

Standard Book Number 8383-1033-8

166560

Printed in the United States of America

CONTENTS.

		PAGE
I.—Darwinism and other Modern Scientific Speculations Reviewed	. . . . .	3
II.—Thomas Carlyle		45
III.—Wit and Humour		91
IV.—Charles Dickens		121
V.—Thomas de Quincey		159
VI.—Modern Civilization, etc.		189
VII.—Heroism: A Lecture		217

ERRATA.

Page 28, line 6, *for* " De Quartefrages " *read* " De Quatrefages."
,, 29, ,, 20, ,, "provision," *read* "prevision."
,, 63, ,, 1, *omit comma after* " England," *insert it after* " too."
,, 97, ,, 18, *for* " truth," *read* " touch."
,, 101, ,, 13, ,, " Mr. Taine," *read* " M. Taine."
,, 116, ,, 8, ,, "contract," *read* "contact."
,, 210, ,, 10, ,, "epiphyses" *read* "epiphysis."
,, 211, ,, 11, ,, "cases," *read* "causes."

DARWINISM,

AND

OTHER MODERN SCIENTIFIC SPECULATIONS

Reviewed.

"Hold thou the good! define it well;
For fear divine Philosophy
Should push beyond her mark, and be
Procuress to the Lords of Hell."

Tennyson.

"In science we find people who can neither see nor hear through sheer learning and hypothesis. It is just because we carry about with us a great apparatus of philosophy and hypothesis that we spoil all.— *Goethe.*

"The man of science ought to go on honestly, patiently, diffidently, observing and storing up his observations, and carrying his reasonings unflinchingly to their legitimate conclusions, convinced that it would be treason to the majesty at once of science and of religion if he sought to help either by swerving ever so little from the straight rule of truth."— *Archbishop Tait.*

Modern Scientific Speculations.

IN studying the speculations of the most advanced scientific men of the present day, it is remarkable how little we find that is new. Even in the most startling hypotheses which have been put forth there is a remarkable parallelism with the speculations of ancient times. Opinions, old as Poetry and Philosophy, are constantly reappearing, in association with modern ideas. And after their long slumber, when reproduced and clad in new forms, they are accepted by many as new. But, inasmuch as they profess to solve some of the great problems, which, in spite of the new light of Modern Science, remain insoluble still, they must not be accepted without challenge.

The longing for certitude, and the earnest desire to solve the great mysteries by which he is surrounded, is at bottom the cause of this constant and earnest striving in man. And though the domain of Physical Science is boundless, and, by our improved methods of observation, there are discoveries to be made and new fields of inquiry to be explored, which require nothing but careful experiment and acuteness of reason to push investigations to their farthest limits; yet there is a certain fascination in plunging into those mysteries which transcend human reason, which only confuse and defy us at every step, and at last lead us into "a land of mists and shadows," and too often into "a wilderness of perplexities and errors." Thus we find that some of the greatest philosophers have also been the greatest dreamers, and, according to Lord Bacon, they have "invented more fables than the poets." For when Reason does dream, her wild-eyed sister, Imagination, is calm and unpretentious in comparison.

Of late years we have, perhaps, seen the truth of this, for we have had theories propounded and questions proposed which have startled us by their audacity. A sensation-age must naturally produce sensation-science, as well as sensation-novels; sensation-philosophy, as well as sensation-poetry; and the fear is that some of our philosophers are losing that sense of reverence which is necessary to purify the mind from egotism, self-assertion, and pride of opinion, and to lead to that which Lord Bacon calls "a blessed humility of mind." "For," says that great philosopher, "it is no less true in this human kingdom of knowledge than in God's kingdom of heaven, that no man shall enter it except he becomes first as a little child." For a right moral sense is as necessary as any mental quality for a clear perception of objective facts, and the laws and principles which inhere in them. "The human understanding' says Bacon, "receives an infusion from the will and affections; so that what a man would most wish to be true, that he most readily believes."

We hope to treat our subject in a Catholic spirit, as we have no predilections we would not willingly exchange for Truth. And all that we require for our present investigation is, not any special scientific knowledge, but only the application of those reasoning powers by which we are able to form a judgment from the evidence of facts before us; or, in other words, the common sense which guides us in the ordinary decisions of life. For if our scientific men give us the facts or data upon which they build an hypothesis, they only supply, as it were, the materials for reasoning; and they have themselves, as they confess, only arrived at a provisional judgment. The arrangement and generalisation of these facts must be verified and their causes determined. They must in truth be transplanted from the external to the intellectual sphere, and during the process care must be taken to keep the speculative assumption apart from the inductive conclusion. For there is a tendency in the present day to give to the mere tentative efforts of some of our philosophical speculatists a scientific weight and authority which they do not possess; and we must remember that true science does not deal with guesses : it asserts and *maintains* that which is capable of proof, and embraces such facts as can be co-ordinated into general formulæ; but an hypothesis, which is often based upon the generalisation of partial facts, and which carries with it only the weight of probability, should be carefully distinguished, and estimated for its real value. It can be used only for suggestion, not for demonstration. Now, an hypothesis is a thing we cannot well grapple with: it is not solid and substantial; it is not wholly fact; it is not wholly fiction. It is a superstructure which is often fair to look at, and which may be admired for the ingenuity that has been displayed in the building (for the imagination is a good architect), but which is, after all, too often but a castle of air.

Now speculation within certain limits is perfectly legitimate and useful. We cannot wholly control the imagination, if we would; and man's discourse of reason will look before and after. And even when the mind is striving after something that is unattainable, much may be acquired that is accessible; for out of Astrology arose Astronomy, out of Alchemy the modern science of Chemistry: and some of the most wonderful discoveries of the present century are but the realization of the dreams of our forefathers. Physical Science has, within the last century, wrought marvels—its discoveries form a new epoch in the world's history. "We are giants in physical power," says Carlyle. "In a deeper than metaphorical sense, we are Titans, that strive, by heaping mountain on mountain, to conquer heaven also."

But, after all, the study of Physical Science is one-sided; and an *exclusive* devotion to physical pursuits, as Sir W. Hamilton has shown, exerts an evil influence upon the mind, and has a tendency to lead the student, if he speculates at all, to Materialism. "Any one study," says Dr. Newman, "of whatever kind, exclusively pursued, deadens in the mind the interest, nay, the perception, of any other." Thus, those who are working only in the visible, are in danger of losing their belief in the invisible.

It is a chronic affection of the English mind to suffer at certain times from Panic; and as a result of our too great devotion to physical pursuits, the panic which has cast its shadow of fear over the intelligent English mind is that of Materialism. We fear that Matter is destroying Mind. This is but a temporary eclipse, which, if we wait patiently, will soon pass away; and we need not imitate the barbarians, who in their panic, with discordant cries and beating of drums, strive to drive away an eclipse from off the face of the sun.

Let us not be afraid of free investigation, but welcome Truth when it appears in any shape, and follow it whithersoever it may lead; for we have nothing to fear from increased knowledge. The grand truths of the world, like the pillars of heaven, support themselves; for truth is great and mighty above all things. "Know ye not," says Milton, "that truth is strong, next to the Almighty? Though all the winds of doctrine were let loose to play upon the earth, so truth be in the field we injure her to misdoubt her strength." To understand the measure of human knowledge, to restrain himself within the limits of the comprehensible—to avoid mixing up science with those questions which can only end in guesses—is the true work of a man of science; for half the controversies upon religion and philosophy are of such a nature as can never be settled; and were we to argue until Doomsday, these questions would remain as unanswered as ever. However daring may be our speculations, we are stopped at the onset by the ignorance which encompasses us as with a cloud: "For mystery is everywhere around us, and in us, under our feet, among our hands."

In entering into the consideration of this subject we may remark that we have to deal only with the *speculations*, and not with the *discoveries*, of our scientific men.

We dare not be so presumptuous as to speak a single word against the legitimate discoveries of science. People may rail at science and philosophy, but the lover of truth will not listen to *railing* but to *reasoning*, and in everything he has mastered he has ever a straightforward decision in acting, which is sure as insight and rapid as instinct. Thus it is related of a celebrated naturalist and philosopher that some students once took it into their heads to play a trick upon him. One of them adopted the cloven foot and horns of a certain mythical personage, and in that disguise went to him at midnight when he was alone to frighten him. "I am the devil," said the figure, "and I am come to eat you up." "I defy you," said the man of science; "cloven foot and horns you are herbivorous, and you cannot do it." Science has discovered the cloven foot, tail, and horns, in many of our myths.

It has been remarked, perhaps a little too triumphantly, that every scientific discovery has to pass through three stages. First, people deny the truth of it; next, it is declared to be contrary to religion, and, therefore, the work of the devil (what a benefactor of the human race this devil has been); and, lastly, it is said that nobody ever denied it. This may be sometimes truly said of the discoveries of our scientific men, but not of their speculations.

It has ever been a dream of the human mind to elaborate from the depth of its nature the secret of its own existence—to solve the greatest of all physiological riddles, the Secret of Life. This is a vain endeavour: for life is a mystery, and man is not capable of explaining his own existence; nor shall we ever be able to say what Life is, and all our attempted explanations fall short of explanation.

"Life," says Herbert Spencer, "is the definite combination of heterogeneous changes, both simultaneous and successive, in correspondence with external coexistences and sequences." This is an explanation which, like all others of the same kind, requires explanation. Professor Huxley has endeavoured, in his article on Protoplasm, to deal with the question of, What is Life? but he has not spanned the chasm which separates Life from Death. "The gulf of all gulfs, that gulf which Mr. Huxley's Protoplasm is as powerless to efface as any other material expedient that has ever been suggested since the eyes of men first looked into it—the mighty gulf between death and life." Life in itself is as great a mystery now as it was in the days of Plato and Aristotle. We know that we exist, although that is denied by some of our modern philosophers. We can define, in some measure, the conditions of our existence; but Life in its essence eludes our grasp: nor shall we ever know, for we cannot dissect a living body. Goethe says,

> "Who seeks to learn, or gives
> Descriptions of, a thing that lives,
> Begins with 'murdering, to dissect'
> The lifeless parts he may inspect—
> The limbs are there beneath his knife
> And all—but that which gives them life."

As with physical, so with moral life—it is a mystery:

"And as to anatomise the body," says Froude, "will not reveal the secret of animation, so with the actions of the moral man. The spiritual life, which alone gives them meaning and being, glides away before the logical dissecting knife, and leaves it but a corpse to work upon."

In passing from the phenomena of Life to those of Mind, we enter a region as profoundly mysterious. "Man," says Pascal, "is to himself the mightiest prodigy of nature, for he is unable to conceive what is body, still less what is mind; but least of all is he able to conceive how a body can be united to a mind—yet this is his proper being." Ontological speculations and the problems of existence remain as inexplicable as ever.

There are many curious speculations as to the origin of Life and Thought. One philosopher has asserted that the principle of Life must be ascribed to a gas. We have been taught to believe that "the inspiration of the Almighty giveth understanding." But one of our modern professors[*] has discovered "that the brain secretes thought, as the liver secretes bile;" and that "poetry and religion are a product of the smaller intestines." Another resolves Thought into a chemical substance, and declares that "Thought is Phosphorus."[†] Another puts forth the astounding Theory that "man is what he eats;"[‡] and it has been suggested "that our successors may even dare to speculate on the changes that converted a crust of bread or a bottle of wine, in the brain of Swift, Molière, or Shakespeare, into the conception of the gentle Glumdal-

---

[*] Dr. Cabanis.   [†] Moleschott.   [‡] Feuerbach.

clitch, the rascally Sganarelle, or the immortal Falstaff," *
in much the same way, we suppose, as Scrooge attributed
the ghost of Marley " to a diseased stomach, to a bit of
indigestible beef, a blot of mustard, or a fragment of
underdone potato."

> "A certain high priest can explain
> How the soul is but nerve at the most,
> And how Milton had glands in his brain
> Which secreted the Paradise Lost."

After disposing of Life and Mind and converting them
both into Matter, some of our Physical Philosophers are
beginning now very politely to bow GOD out of the
universe: for none but a Philosopher can reason away
the existence of a Maker. "Your God impedes you,"
says an eminent Frenchman. "He is the Supreme Cause,
and you dare not reason on Causes out of respect for
Him. He is the most important personage in England,
and I see clearly that He merits His position, for He
forms part of your Constitution. He is the Guardian of
your morality. He judges in final appeal on all questions
whatsoever. He replaces with advantage the prefects and
gendarmes with whom the nations on the Continent are
still encumbered. Yet this high rank has the incon-
venience of all official positions—it produces a cant, prejudice, intolerance, and courtiers."

We notice the half-apologetic way in which some
scientific men introduce the idea of a Creator, as if He
had been disposed of; and the argument of Paley as to
the evidence of a Creator from design was obsolete; but

---

* Professor Haughton.

Paley's arguments, although they may be old, are yet unanswered: and it is much easier to put forth new questions than answer old arguments—to start paradoxes than make discoveries. And in the present time there is a danger of our committing the folly of the servant in the story of "Aladdin"—of being deceived by the cry of new lamps for old.

One of the favourite hypotheses put forward by the most advanced Physical Philosophers of the present day is that of Natural Evolution, by which they seek to arrive at a single source of power from which all vital energy is derived; and the God of this world they would teach us is the Sun. "It is now considered proved," says Professor Tyndall, "that all the energy which we derive from plants and animals is drawn from the sun; that there is no creative energy whatever in the vegetable or animal organism; but that all the power which we obtain from the muscles of men and animals, as much as that which we develop by the combustion of wood or coal, has been produced at the sun's expense." And here we have the origin of the world according to this gospel of Modern Science. "Supposing," says the same author, "a planet carved from the Sun and set spinning round an axis, and revolving round the Sun at a distance from him equal to that of our earth, would one of the consequences of its refrigeration be the development of organic forms? I lean to the affirmative." And again, in defining the hypothesis of Natural Evolution, he says — "Not alone the more ignoble forms of animalcula or animal life, not alone the nobler forms of horse and lion, not alone the exquisite and wonderful mechanism of the human body, but that human mind itself—emotion, intellect, will, and all their phenomena—were once latent in a fiery cloud." So that, according to this theory, we are to believe that the mind of Plato and Shakespeare had a potential existence in a nebulous particle in some remote period of time.

No doubt one of the great objects of Modern Science is to bring together, and connect under common laws, phenomena seemingly the most remote and dissimilar, to reduce to as small a number as possible, the many forms of matter which are elementary to our present knowledge, and to show their mutual convertibility. All science tends to this unity. And the great doctrine of "The Correlation of Physical Forces" seems to confirm the opinions of many scientific men, that the various forms under which the forces of matter are made manifest have one common origin, that beyond the veil of phenomena there is but one force. But, assuming this, "can we," says Sir W. Grove, "suggest a proposition definitely conceivable to the mind, of force without antecedent force? I cannot, without calling for the interposition of creative power, any more than I can conceive the sudden appearance of a mass of matter come from nowhere and formed from nothing." So, if mind has been evolved from matter, it must first of all have been involved; and, if so, it implies "an antecedent cause" or originating mind, which some of the extreme advocates of natural evolution deny.

We cannot understand how we can escape from what Professor Huxley calls "the materialistic slough," which is verily a "Slough of Despond," if we accept a theory of Natural Evolution, which teaches us that all organized beings owe their existence to physical agents, and that not merely life, but even volition and consciousness, are only physical manifestations, so that even God Himself is lost, as a creative being, in the matter which He has evolved. Now in creating, the hardest thing is to begin, and the difficulty of the beginning stares us in the face, even when we bring our Speculations down to the lowest potential atom or existence. Science teaches us that "all animals, without exception, high or low, of whatever ultimate complexity or simplicity of structure, originate from eggs, and from eggs of the same character," and this fact is one of the chief arguments against spontaneous generation, for the egg is the primary germ. What is called gemmiparity, or the faculty of reproducing by buds, and fissiparity or reproduction by cuttings, whether spontaneous or artificial, in the lowest forms of animal life are only subordinate functions, for after a certain period the sexes reappear and give birth to eggs, so that oviparous reproduction is the only fundamental one. The problem which puzzled the old philosophers remains the same now as then. They asked the question, Which was the first in the beginning, the hen or the egg? We cannot, they said, get the hen without the egg, or get the egg without the hen. The same difficulty which applied to the hen applies to all other animals. And when our little systems have had their day and "like streaks of morning cloud" melt away "into the infinite azure of the past" the physical philosophers of the future will be just as near solving the problem of the egg as the philosophers of the past and present. As the creation of the world to many of our professors "is little more mysterious than the cooking of a dumpling," it may be interesting to know, "How were the apples got in?" A late President of the British Association of Science startled us with a bit of sensational cosmogony or biology. Life, according to his theory, might have been born on this earth through the fall of some moss-covered aerolite from some shattered planet, which might even have on it some living animal. "It is so hard," says an American author, "to prove a negative, that if a man should assert that the moon was in truth a green cheese, formed by the coagulable substance of the Milky Way, and challenge me to prove the contrary, I might be puzzled." Swift describes Wisdom as a "hen whose cackling we must value and consider, because it is attended with an egg." And is this moss-covered aerolite the egg which the wisdom of Modern Science has given us to hatch a world? Professor Huxley, in speaking of some of the speculations of geologists, well says that "Men of science, like young colts in a fresh pasture, are apt to be exhilarated on being turned into a new field of inquiry, and to go off at a hand-gallop, in total disregard of hedges and ditches, losing sight of the real limitation of their inquiries, and to forget the extreme imperfection of what is really known. Geologists have imagined that they could tell us what was going on at all parts of the earth's surface during a given epoch; they have talked of this deposit being contemporaneous with that deposit, until, from our little local histories of the changes at limited spots of the earth's surface, they have constructed a universal history of the globe, as full of wonders and portents as any other story of antiquity."

Referring to some of the modern theories of life and of the origin of the earth, we were taught that the universe is but a vast moving machine, self-supported and self-sustained, and that this is a forsaken and fatherless world. Is the time coming which Lichtenberg prophesied in bitter irony, "when belief in God will be as tales with which old women frighten children?" when, in the language of Richter, "of the world will be made a machine, of the æther a gas, of God a force, and of the second world a coffin." And are we to believe, with Mr. Mill, "that a religion may exist without belief in God; and that a religion without a God may be even to Christians an instructive and profitable object of contemplation?" And is this the millennium we are to look forward to "when the faith in a personal God is extinguished, when prayer and praise are no longer to be heard, when the belief is universal that with the body dies the soul; then the false morals of theology will no longer lead the mind astray."* Holding such a creed might not that arch pessimist, Schopenhauer, well describe "Life as a cheat, and a uselessly interrupting episode in the blissful repose of nothing." We do not fear these doctrines making any great impression in this country. Englishmen may go back to Roman Catholicism, or become converted to Mahommedanism or Buddhism, but they are not likely to accept such a creed of negations. And there is one consolation in these and the like speculations. As their

---

* Winwood Reade.

authors have descended into the lowest depths of scepticism and materialism it is to be hoped that, as they can no lower go, they will begin to ascend into the regions of life, light, and immortality.

Physical Science is wholly incompetent to deal with man's moral and spiritual nature. There is a science of Mind as well as a science of Physics. These sciences, as Lord Bacon has well shown, are distinct. For in the analysis of Matter you cannot reach Mind, so from Mind you cannot reach Matter. The Physicist recognizes physical facts, the Metaphysician moral and spiritual facts. One deals with the objective, the other with the subjective. If there is a spiritual life there must be spiritual facts, and the verification of these facts must be from *within*, and not from *without*. Now, Faraday, as a scientific man, recognized both. But Professor Huxley speaks as a man of science, and only as such, when he says, "That the man of science has learned to believe in justification, not by faith, but by verification." The truth is, we must render unto Science the things that belong to Science, and to Faith the things that belong to Faith.

It behoves us, with all due humility, to sit at the feet of our modern Physicist when he instructs us in Natural Philosophy, and imparts to us his discoveries relating to light, heat, and the laws of Matter and Force; but when he leaves these positive teachings, or connects them with speculations which cannot be verified by induction, with some new theory of creation, or no creation, the origin of life, the impossibility of miracles, or the denial of Providence, he changes his relation at once with us; and though we are bound to accept his discoveries, we are free to accept or discard his theories: and we often feel that Newton's reproof to the sceptical Dr. Halley, the great mathematician, might well be applied to some of our modern speculatists. "I always attend to you, Dr. Halley," said Newton, "with the greatest deference, when you do us the honour to converse on astronomy or the mathematics, because these are subjects that you have industriously investigated, and which you well understand; but religion is a subject on which I always hear you with pain, because this is a subject which you have not seriously examined, and do not comprehend: you despise it, because you have not studied it; and you will not study it, because you despise it."

One thing we can anticipate with confidence, in looking at the present strife and conflict of opinions, that truth can never be at variance with truth; it may be in appearance, but not in reality; and it is only a science, "falsely so called," which is antagonistic to true religion; and it is also only a false religion which is opposed to true science.

There ought not rightly to be any collision between science and religion, for they are each separate and independent of one another; as well apply the differential calculus to metaphysics, or study history by the aid of mathematics, or formulate a code of morals upon physics, as explain theology by science, or, what is still worse, explain science by theology. "Physics beware of metaphysics," was the warning cry of Newton; and the same words may apply to theology as well as to metaphysics. Religion is based upon revelation, not upon anything man could have found out for himself. This truth was expressed many years ago by St. Bernard. "The objects of faith," said he, "are given us from above; they are revealed by God, exactly because it is impossible they should be discovered by man." Nature, by her own light, will never reveal herself; and science, by itself, can only raise altars to an "unknown god," and re-echo the sublime words which were inscribed upon the ancient Temple of Isis (the great mother—Nature): " I am whatsoever is—whatsoever has been—whatsoever shall be; and the veil which is over my countenance no mortal hand has ever raised." Let science go on increasing in depth and breadth, let human culture go on advancing, so that man shall be fit for his place here, but let it be left to religion to perfect him and make him fit for heaven.

Perhaps it would be well to notice here what some of our philosophers, in attempting to sweep away what they call "the cobwebs of old theological creeds," would put in their place. Comte, the author of "The Positive Philosophy," after inaugurating a new philosophy which destroys our hope in God and immortality, proceeded to establish a *new religion* of his own, of which he was the self-constituted high priest (knowing, as he did, that man must have a religion of some kind), the worship of which has been attempted somewhere in London. Mr. Mill has given us a *résumé* of what that religion is. It is a deification of his own system of science and sociology. He had no God, but he had a *grand être* in collective humanity, or "the continuous resultant of all forces capable of voluntarily concurring in the universal perfectioning of the world;" and as woman is the perfection of humanity, the worship of *woman* is the highest object of his adoration.

The objects of private adoration are the *mother*, the *wife*, and the *daughter*, representing severally the past, the present, and the future, and calling into active exercise the three social sentiments, veneration, attachment, and kindness. We are to regard them, whether dead or alive, as our guardian angels. If the last two have never existed, or if in the particular case any of the three types is too faulty for the office assigned to it, the place may be supplied by some other type of womanly excellence, even by one merely historical.

M. Comte incorporates into the ideal object whose service is to be the law of our life, not only our *own species*, but in a subordinate degree, our humble auxiliaries, those *animal races* which enter into real society with men, which attach themselves to him, and voluntarily co-operate with him, like the noble dog who gives his life for his human friend and benefactor.

M. Comte is the Philosopher Mr. G. H. Lewis calls "The Bacon of the nineteenth century," a Philosopher whom Mr. Mill delights to honour. If such a religion as this, which has no higher object than the worship of humanity and descends to the worship of the lower animals, is an outcome of the philosophy of the nineteenth century, well might the poet exclaim, "I thank God that I am a *man*, and not a *philosopher*."

But even M. Comte has been outdone by some of the German philosophers. Feuerbach is the leader of another school of mankind worshippers, and this last superstition is called Anthropolatry. "Man alone," says he, "is the true Saviour. Man alone is our God, our judge, our redeemer." By the side of this school there is another, teaching what is called Autolatry or self worship. "Each one," says Max Stirner, " is to himself his own God." This is a very old form of idolatry, and can hardly require some hundred pages of nauseous phraseology to explain and prove. We notice this difference between the "old theological creeds" and these new doctrines which are presumptuously called scientific : in the former God creates Man ; in the latter Man creates God.

Passing by speculations which have gone into the eternal limbo of forgotten things, we come now to notice the theory of Natural Selection, by which Mr. Darwin has endeavoured to trace the origin and progress of life from its lowest forms up to man. Mr. Darwin has devoted years of study and research in collecting facts to prove his theory. He has written books which are full of interest and are valuable as contributions to Natural History. He has accumulated an enormous number of facts, but these must not be mistaken for arguments, for facts always may be brought forward to support any theory. "And the human mind," says Bacon, "when it has once got hold of any notion, or supposed principle, is given to make *all* the facts it afterwards meets with accord with that, and lend it their support. It is also much more easily moved and excited by affirmatives than by negatives, that is, by instances that seem to support its preconceived notions, than by such as seem to be opposed to them." We shall endeavour to explain what is Mr. Darwin's theory of Natural Selection, and to use his own words as nearly as we can. Nature, he affirms, in successive generations gives varieties (in fact, each living creature produced differs, to some extent, from every other of its kind). These varieties, in the struggle for existence, have unequal fortune; those individuals in which the variations are of a favourable character, will be more vigorous; those most adapted to the circumstances of the time and place prosper, and give origin to descendants, which run the same risks, but which, under the principle of what Mr. Darwin calls "Natural Selection," acquire more and more the character of distinctness and superiority. In this struggle the weakest, in common phrase, goes to the wall, and there is what Herbert Spencer calls "The survival of the fittest." The theory of Natural Selection is the doctrine of Malthus applied to the animal and vegetable world; a struggle for existence inevitably follows, owing to the tendency to geometrical increase of all kinds of animals and plants; and as more individuals are produced than can possibly survive, those individuals having any advantage, however slight over others, will have the best chance of surviving and of procreating their kind, while, on the other hand, any variation in the least degree injurious will be rigidly destroyed.

Mr. Darwin maintains the doctrine that species are not immutable. "Although much remains obscure," says he, "and will long remain obscure, I can entertain no doubt, after the most deliberate study and most dispassionate judgment of which I am capable, that the view which most naturalists entertain, and which I formerly entertained, namely, that each species has been independently created, is erroneous. I am fully convinced that species are not immutable, but that those belonging to what are called the same genera are lineal descendants of some other and generally extinct species, in the same way as the acknowledged varieties of any one species are the descendants of that species."

In answer to the questions, "How is it that varieties which he calls incipient species become ultimately converted into good and distinct species, which in most cases obviously differ from each other far more than do the varieties of the same species?"—" How do those groups of species which constitute what are called distinct genera, and which differ from each other more than do the species of the same genus, arise?" he says, "All these results follow from the struggle for life. Owing to this struggle, variations, however slight, and from whatever cause proceeding, if they be in any degree profitable to the individuals of a species, in their infinitely complex relations to other organic beings and to their physical conditions of life, will tend to the preservation of such individuals, and will generally be inherited by the offspring. The offspring, also, will thus have a better chance of surviving; for of the many individuals of any species which are periodically born but a small number can survive. I have called this principle, by which each slight variation, if useful, is preserved, by the term Natural Selection, in order to mark its relation to man's power of selection. But the expression often used by Mr. Herbert Spencer of the Survival of the Fittest is more accurate, and is sometimes equally convenient. We have seen that man by selection can certainly produce great results, and can adapt organic beings to his own uses, through the accumulation of slight but useful variations given to him by the hand of Nature. But Natural Selection is a power incessantly ready for action, and is immeasurably superior to man's feeble efforts, as the works of Nature are to those of Art."

Breaking down the barrier of species, Mr. Darwin has endeavoured to deduce all the varieties of life that now are on the earth; not only those of insects, birds, fishes, beasts, but those also of man, from a few forms of life, or from one primordial germ.

In accounting for these great changes, Mr. Darwin falls back upon "unlimited periods of time." Now time is recognised in other physical sciences as an essential element of natural operations; but Mr. Darwin does not leave us even a guess in respect to how long a period it takes to modify a species, as he cannot point to any modification during the last several thousand years. He confesses, also, that many animals have remained unchanged since the commencement of the glacial period, "and these have been exposed to great changes of climate, and have migrated over great distances."

If the theory of Natural Selection is true, Geology ought to furnish the most valuable and complete evidence in its support. But Mr. Darwin acknowledges that some of the facts of Geology are nearly fatal to his theory; and in order to surmount these difficulties, he lays great stress on the imperfection of the geological record. In the lowest known fossiliferous rocks "are found species belonging to several of the main divisions of the animal kingdom;" and Mr. Darwin says, that if his theory is true, "it is indisputable that before the lowest Cambrian stratum was deposited, long periods elapsed, as long as, or probably far longer than the whole interval from the Cambrian age to the present day, and that during these vast periods the world swarmed with living creatures."

Now Geology at present gives us no evidence of these vast periods, and Mr. Darwin acknowledges the almost entire absence as at present known of formations rich in fossils beneath the Cambrian stratum.

The next order of fossiliferous rocks is the Silurian. These rocks abound with oceanic life, which has been well preserved, but there are no fish. Next in geological succession is the Devonian, when suddenly appear fish of the highest and most perfect type. "In short," says Sir R. Murchison, "the first created fish, like the first forms of those other orders, was just as marvellously constructed as the last which made its appearance, or is now living, in our seas." Between those two great classes of the Mollusca and the fishes, there is no trace of any transitional forms, although the minutest organisms have been preserved. But, if life had been gradually developed from one or more primordial forms, surely the geologist ought to be able to arrange the fossil remains in a real though broken series, so as to form a few links in this long chain of easy graduated life, however imperfect might be the geological record.

The continued operation of natural laws in the production of all organisms have always been noticed by naturalists and others, but Mr. Darwin was the first to give the term Selection exclusively to the action of those causes which are for ever shaping and modifying all animated and organic existences; and many centuries ago, even as far back as the time of Aristotle, the argument of "The survival of the fittest" was discussed and reasoned out by those wise men of old.

Natural Selection, as put forth by Mr. Darwin, is a Providence without a God. He speaks of it as not only altering, but he attributes to it a creative power, involving the addition of new bones or new organs. Now, supposing Mr. Darwin's theory can account for the difference in the structure of an animal—the lengthening of the giraffe's neck, for instance, which may have been acquired by the original animal having been impelled by a succession of dearths to seek its food in the branches of trees, and thus to have extended its neck by constant use—can it, even within the infinite time required, by any outward conditions account for the various organs with which the higher animals are endowed? How can it account, for instance, by numerous successive slight modifications for all the complex mechanism of the eye and ear. "Did light," says Dr. Stirling, "or did the pulsations of the air, even by any length of time, indent into the sensitive cell, eyes and a pair of eyes—ears and a pair of ears? Light, conceivably, might shine for ever without such a wonderfully complicated result as an eye. Similarly, for delicacy and marvellous ingenuity of structure, the ear is scarcely inferior to the eye; and surely it is possible to think of a whole infinitude of those fitful and fortuitous air tremblings, which we call sound, without indentation into anything whatever of such an organ."

According to Lucretius, The eyes were not made to see with, but being formed by a 'fortuitous concurrence of atoms,' men, finding them well adapted for the purpose of seeing, used them as such. For, says he, if eyes were made to see with, then seeing must have existed before eyes; and if seeing existed before eyes, what could be the use of eyes? And if seeing did not exist before eyes, how could eyes be made for that which is not—in other words, for nothing? Clearly, then, eyes were not made to see with. In some of the philosophical speculations of the nineteenth century there is often a great flavour of this hypothetical reasoning of Lucretius.

We cannot help being driven to the conclusion respecting Mr. Darwin's theory, that, as it is now presented to us, though worked out with wonderful ingenuity and with almost boundless resources of knowledge, it is very far from proven. He cannot bring forward one single case of the transmutation of species. After all the experiments he has made on pigeons, by careful selection and breeding a pigeon is a pigeon still. And there is no doubt that, in common with other domestic animals, if these pigeons were turned back again to their wild state, they would have no power to transmit the bias they have received from careful selection and breeding, and that in a few generations their progeny would revert to their own original form. There is a special provision for the protection of some animals which Natural Selection cannot by any means account for, and which seems to annul the idea of primitive community of species. We allude to the several forms of bodily apparatus which some animals possess, such as electric fishes, the poison of serpents, and also those curious cases of mimicry in insects, noticed by Mr. Mivart in his admirable book, "The Genesis of Species."

So far as we have the evidence of facts, it does not

support the hypothesis of indefinite variability; for there seems to be a certain limit in which the production of certain degrees of abnormality in individuals, when once attained, cannot be further increased; and this is shown, perhaps, in the distinction between species and race. The former, observes Professor De Quatrefages, is the proper recognition of original organic differences; the latter marks merely the minor differences which have arisen under different circumstances of development, and which can be resolved back again into the original type. For instance, the wild turkey of North America, of deep brown, iridescent colour, is the parent of all the varied types of the domestic breed, both in Europe and America. When released from the influence of domestication, and turned into the forest, this bird reverts to its original type. The different breeds of turkeys, then, constitute examples of races. Species embraces all the different races. Different species are separated by fundamental differences of constitution, which render their copulative union infertile, except in a few isolated cases — such as the horse and the ass and a few others; but in all cases the hybrid are incapable of reproduction. Races, on the contrary, *thrive* by crossing, not only producing by their unions higher organisms, but also developing a higher reproductive power. *Fertility*, then, is the law of union between races; infertility marks unions between species.

Professor Huxley, though an ardent supporter of the theory of Evolution, says: "After much consideration, and with assuredly no bias against Mr. Darwin's views, it is our clear conviction that, as the evidence stands, it is not absolutely proven that a group of animals, having all the characters exhibited by species in Nature, has ever been originated by selection, whether artificial or natural."

Agassiz says also, "Had Mr. Darwin or his followers furnished *a single fact* to show that individuals change in the course of time, in such a manner as to produce at last species different from those known before, the state of the case might be different. But it stands recorded now, as before, that the animals known to the ancients are still in existence, exhibiting to this day the characters they exhibited of old. Until the facts of nature are shown to have been mistaken by those who have collected them, and that they have a different meaning from that now generally assigned to them, I shall therefore consider the transmutation theory as a scientific mistake, *untrue* in its facts, *unscientific* in its methods, and *mischievous* in its tendency."

But granting the principle of Natural Selection to be true, that species undergo advantageous modifications during a long course of descent, may not these which are called accidental causes be under the direction of an all-provident mind? Is it not reasonable to suppose that in natural, as well as in artificial selection, there is choice and guidance? Man in his selection chooses two factors, both of them possessing the characteristic features he wants to obtain. Must there not be some design, or provision in nature, which gives similar results to those obtained only by man's thoughtful and well directed industry through domestication, "and which," as Mr. Darwin says, "works solely by and for the good of each being?" Mr. Darwin denies this special guidance, for he says, "No shadow of reason can be assigned for the belief that the variations, alike in nature and the result of the same general laws, which have been the groundwork, through Natural Selection, of the formation of the most perfectly adapted animals in the world, man included, were intentionally and specially guided." We cannot so far follow Mr. Darwin, nor understand why his theory should banish the principle of finality, or that it should be used by most of his followers as a peremptory argument against final causes. Nor can we see that it is logically inconsistent with the views held by the majority of teleologists. Since the publication of his views upon Natural Selection, Mr. Darwin has grown bolder, and as his theory has now, he says, made good its claims to acceptance, he no longer hesitates to push it to its final conclusion. That conclusion is clear and definite. It is, that "Man, the wonder and glory of the universe," is, to use his own words, "descended from a hairy quadruped, furnished with a tail and pointed ears, probably arboreal in its habits, and an inhabitant of the Old World. This creature, if its whole structure had been examined by a naturalist, would have been classed amongst the Quadrumana, as surely as would the common and still more ancient progenitor of the Old and New World monkeys. The Quadrumana and all the higher mammals are probably derived from an ancient marsupial animal, and this through a long line of diversified forms, either from some reptile-like or some amphibian-like creature, and this again from some fish-like animal. In the dim obscurity of the past we can see that the early progenitor of all the vertebrata *must* have been an aquatic animal, provided with branchiæ, with the two sexes united in the same individual, and with the most important organs of the body (such as the brain and heart) imperfectly developed. This animal seems to have been more like the larvæ of our existing marine ascidians than any other known form."

Here we have, indeed, a long line of descent for man; and had one of our late proud and aristocratic dukes lived in the present age, he would not in the conceit of his rank and long line of forefathers have declared that "he sincerely pitied Adam because he had no ancestors," and the grand old gardener and his wife might, indeed, in the words of a modern poet, "smile at the claims of long descent"—a descent which, Mr. Darwin says, "man ought not to be ashamed of."

As it may be interesting to know something about our early progenitors, we will give Mr. Darwin's account of these ascidians.

"The ascidians are marine creatures permanently attached to a support. They hardly appear like animals, and consist of a simple tough leathery sac, with two small projecting orifices. They have recently been placed by some naturalists amongst the Vermes, or worms. Their larvæ somewhat resemble tadpoles in shape, and have the power of swimming freely about."

There is a remarkable and unique fact respecting these ascidians. It is that they possess a heart which, after having beat a certain number of times, stops, and then beats the opposite way, so as to reverse the course of the current, which returns by-and-bye to its original direction.

"The GREATEST difficulty," says Mr. Darwin, "which presents itself, when we are driven to the above conclusion on the origin of Man, is the high standard of intellectual power, and of the moral disposition which he has attained." Yet to this, his greatest difficulty, he gives in his book but a few pages' consideration. He has brought forward a number of facts to prove the similarity of the human frame and that of animals. But proximity is not identity. For Man's individuality is asserted by his unlikeness to the lower animals. If there is so little difference in body why is there so vast a difference in mind? "For after all," says Plato, "it is the mind which makes the man." As far as regards intelligence the dog is much nearer to man than the ape. If Mr. Darwin's theory is true, our study of humanity must be made entirely from another stand-point. We must regard him, not as a "little lower than the angels," but as a little higher than the beast. Instead of studying him in his highest and noblest attributes we must trace him downwards, evolving slowly from a dot of animated jelly. If Science repudiates miracles, what a miracle is this! If Faith has its enigmas, what enigmas are here! Mr. Darwin finds his theory of Natural Selection when applied to Man imperfect, and he has added another important agency, or, we might say, he has developed a new theory, which he calls "Sexual Selection;" for he now acknowledges that in his former works "he attributed too much to the action of Natural Selection." These chapters on Sexual Selection are very interesting in themselves; for we have a minute account of the "loves of insects," "the loves of fishes, of birds, and of mammals," reminding us of his grandfather, who wrote a poem on "The Loves of the Plants" and who

Modern Scientific Speculations Reviewed. 33

also had his curious speculations on the origin of Life. One of his speculations was "that the first insects were the anthers or the stigmas of flowers, which had by some means loosed themselves from their parent plant, and that many other insects have in long process of time been formed from these, some acquiring wings, others claws, and others fins, from their ceaseless efforts to procure their food, or to secure themselves from injury."

Nursed in such speculations as these, it is no wonder that his grandson should have inherited the same ideas, and, with his far greater scientific knowledge, should have pushed his theories in the same direction. As we said before, Mr. Darwin has but briefly treated that part of his subject which points to the great distinction between man and the lower animals, viz., in the higher mental qualities of "abstraction, individuality, and self-consciousness." Mr. Darwin evades this difficulty by saying that "it would be useless to attempt discussing these higher qualities, which, according to several recent writers, make the sole and complete distinction between man and the brutes, for hardly two authors agree in their definitions." This mode of reasoning is most unsatisfactory and unscientific. For he looks almost exclusively upon the animal side of man's nature, and nearly loses sight of what chiefly distinguishes him from the lower animals—his moral and religious sentiments. And if man has a soul, with all its glorious attributes, it would be interesting to know, according to Mr. Darwin's theory, how he became possessed of it. Did he acquire it by Natural or Sexual Selection? This is a question Mr.

Darwin does not once raise, much less attempt to solve.

The highest and noblest attributes of man are attributed to mere animal instincts. For instance, he does not rest morality upon any immutable laws—his conceptions of right and wrong are based upon instinctive impulses, which vary according to circumstances. "If," says he, to take an extreme case, "men were reared under precisely the same conditions as hive bees, there can be no doubt that our unmarried females would, like the working bees, think it a sacred duty to kill their brothers, and mothers would strive to kill their fertile daughters, and no one would think of interfering." And yet after this Mr. Darwin can quote with admiration Kant's words —"Duty! wondrous thought, that workest neither by fond insinuation, flattery, nor by any threat, but merely by holding up the naked law in the soul, and so extorting for thyself always reverence, if not always obedience; before which all appetites are dumb, however secretly they rebel."

Mr. Darwin admits that the difference between the mental powers of men and of all other animals is enormous, even when we contrast the mind of one of the lowest savages with that of the most highy organized ape; and, according to Mr. Wallace, "the brain of the savage is vastly superior to any of the lower animals in size and complexity; and this brain gives him, in an undeveloped state, faculties which he never requires to use." "The savage," says Dr. Reid, "hath within him the seeds of the logician, the man of taste and breeding, the orator, the statesman, the man of virtue, and the saint. Nature hath planted the seeds in our minds, and left the rearing of them to human culture." Mr. Darwin would seem to admit this, for he says—"The Fuegians rank among the lowest barbarians, but I was continually struck with surprise how closely the three natives on board H.M.'s ship 'Beagle,' who had lived some years in England, and could talk a little English, resembled us in disposition, and in most of our mental faculties."

"Man alone," says Archbishop Sumner, "is capable of progressive improvement." The savage, when young, is susceptible of educational influences; you can make a reasonable being of him, but try to educate a young monkey, and if Mr. Darwin's theory is true, this might be worthy of the consideration of our School Boards. And if we cannot educate them, how did they educate one another? Sydney Smith humorously says—" I feel so sure that the blue ape without a tail will never rival us in poetry, painting, and music, that I see no reason whatever why justice may not be done to the few fragments of soul and tatters of understanding which they may really possess. I have sometimes felt a little uneasy at Exeter 'Change from contrasting the monkeys with the 'prentice boys who are teasing them; but a few pages of Locke, or a few lines of Milton, have always restored me to tranquillity, and convinced me that the superiority of man had nothing to fear." Respecting language, Mr. Darwin says that the mental powers in some early progenitors of man must have been more highly developed than in any existing ape before the most imperfect form of speech could have come into use. For he admits that there can be no language without thought. Now, this is the missing link. Where is the trace of these intermediate animals? They belong only to his imagination. For science at present gives us no more trace of any such individuals than it does of the vile conception of the race of Yahoos, which emanated from Swift's brain, unless we go back and give credence to some of the monsters we find in Pliny's Natural History, where, among other wonders, he describes some of the fables of Grecian travellers, "such as the existence of headless and mouthless men, men with only one foot, and men with very long ears;" and if they ever existed, they must have shared the fate of the Kilkenny cats, without leaving even a vestige of their tails.

Now, according to the principle of Natural Selection, some of these races ought to have survived. How is it that the monkey survives while "a series of forms graduating insensibly from some ape-like creature to man," are destroyed? According to his hypothesis, the strongest should survive; according to his facts the strongest have perished.

It is in these higher mental qualities, which Mr. Darwin nearly ignores, we place the wide and impassable gulf between man and the brute, which science at present cannot bridge over. And the question arises: Is the savage the original or the degenerate man? Is the rude maker of flint implements the original being into whose nostrils was breathed "the breath of life"—the man whom we have been taught was created in the image of his Maker? And the question to be solved also is this: Did man acquire the moral and religious sense through his animal nature, or was it implanted in him by a higher power? We consider the presence of a moral sense in ourselves presumes a moral nature in the power which has called us into existence: "For it is impossible to conceive," says Carlyle, "that these high faculties should have been put into us by a being that has none of its own;" and as "man did not create himself, so we think he did not instruct himself."

Now poets and philosophers, both ancient and modern, have speculated on the origin of man; and his heaven-born origin is to be found in the mythologies and religions of most people, where we find traditions of a better time, *before* man became degenerate. We can trace this tradition in those strange Eastern nations, whose speculations seem to antedate all historic record; also in the graceful fantasies of the Greek poets and philosophers, for we read in Plato "of a most ancient people, men better than we, and dwelling nigh to the Gods." We find also in the clear-cut brilliancy of the Roman poets, in the writings of Virgil and Ovid, traditions of what was called "the golden age." Of course, it will be said that this is but tradition and poetry. But one of the most logical and scientific thinkers of the present day, Professor Max Müller, has helped to confirm the truth of these traditions by the light of Comparative Philology—a science which, by the classification of language and a careful analysis of words, has shed a dazzling light into the darkest ages of the history of man. Now one thing is certain, we cannot trace our descent, or, more properly speaking, our ascent from savages; for we have no evidence that the lake-dwellers of Switzerland, or the flint-hatchet makers of Abbeville, were our ancestors.

But one thing we do know, that we are descended from the great Aryan Family which emigrated from North-Western Asia; and whether we accept the truth of divine revelation or not as to the origin of man, we cannot deny, that it is from the east we trace the first signs of man having the divine gift and the use of reason, and that it is from this great Aryan Family the world owes its civilization and progress. Professor Max Müller has given us a very interesting sketch of this great family before it separated, and spread over Asia and Europe; and we know something of the habits of life, state of thought, language, religion, and civilization of these our great and remote ancestors; and in these investigations we are carried back to times "before a single Greek or German reached the shores of Europe, or before a single Brahmin descended into the plains of India. And as far as we can trace back the footsteps of man, even on the lowest strata of history, we see that the divine gift of a sound and sober intellect belonged to him from the first, and the idea of a humanity emerging slowly from the depths of animal brutality can never be maintained again." The same learned Professor says also, "That it is a remarkable fact, which no one would venture to doubt, that the supreme deity of the Greeks and the Germans is called by the same name as the supreme deity of these earliest Aryan settlers in India. Does not this fact draw away the curtain from the dark ages of antiquity, and open before our eyes an horizon which we can hardly measure by years?" We need not remark that the conclusion arrived at by Max Müller, viz., the divine source of religion, is in contradiction of Mr. Darwin's theory, which ascribes the religious sentiments in man to the rude fears and frightful dreams of the lowest savages.

So far as we can see within historic time, the world remains nearly the same; situations are repeated; one people lives, loves, and feels like another; and men in the earliest recorded times have been our equals, if not our superiors, in intellectual power. In philosophy we have never excelled Plato; and our art of reasoning is not much improved since Aristotle formulated his system of logic. In poetry we have not advanced beyond David and Homer; and in modern times it would be vain to seek for a greater mathematician than Euclid, or to compare modern eloquence with Demosthenes and Cicero; and we must remember that our earliest records are scanty, for when the Alexandrian library was burnt, half a world was lost. Now by Natural Selection we cannot account for, say, a Homer or an Aristotle; or, in more modern times, a Chaucer or a Shakespeare;—these men did not come by gradual development; and if near 3000 years has made no difference in man, why should we suppose that 10,000 or 100,000 years, or the unlimited time Mr. Darwin requires for his hypothesis, would do so? It is impossible to say what might or might not have been during periods so vast that we have no record of them. But into this unknown region Mr. Darwin boldly enters, and builds up the whole of his theory; and the way in which he draws his ultimate conclusion is very unsatisfactory, he says, "That man was certainly descended from an ape." But how does he arrive at that conclusion? "Not," says the *Times,* " by the proper scientific mood, the indicative, for science tells us what has been, what is, and what will be: but Mr. Darwin's argument is a continuous conjugation of the potential mood; it rings the changes on 'can have been,' 'might have been,' 'would have been,' until it leaps with a bound into 'must have been.' This is not the line of reasoning by which we arrive at a certainty.

We have now considered some of the difficulties which met us in studying Mr. Darwin's book on the "Descent of Man:" there are many others in relation to Geology, Physiology, and Astronomy, which we cannot examine now. We have confined ourselves rather to those general and fundamental objections which forbid our acceptance of his theory as it now stands.

In concluding this survey, perhaps some people will say that these doctrines of Mr. Darwin are perfectly harmless; and the best way is to let them alone, because they will never reach the common mind. We do not think so; for "Opinions," it has been said, "like showers, are generated in high places; but they invariably descend into low ones, and ultimately flow down to the people, as the rains unto the sea." And we can conceive of a tribe of dunces, who never had more than one thought in their lives, and that a foolish one, reading just enough of Mr. Darwin's book to misunderstand him, but who will at once claim relationship with the monkey, and by the impudence of self-assertion, the audacity of intellectual littleness, and the foppery of self-conceit, almost justify their claim to such a descent; and muddling his theory with Atheism, or some other foolish "ism," will seek to convert others as weak and vain as themselves.

"We wish," says the *Times*, in concluding a review of

Mr. Darwin's *Descent of Man*, "we could think that these speculations were as innocuous as they are unpractical and unscientific, but it is too probable that if unchecked they might exert a very mischievous influence. We abstain from noticing their bearings on religious thought, though it is hard to see how, on Mr. Darwin's hypothesis, it is possible to ascribe to man any other immortality, or any other spiritual existence, than that possessed by the brutes. But apart from these considerations, if such views as he advances on the nature of the moral sense were generally accepted, it seems evident that morality would lose all elements of stable authority, and the ever fixed marks around which the tempests of human passion now break themselves would cease to exert their guiding and controlling influence. Men, unfortunately, have the power of acting, not according to what is their ultimate social interest, but according to their ideas of it; and if the doctrine could be impressed on them, that right and wrong have no other meaning than the pursuit or the neglect of that ultimate interest, conscience would cease to be a check upon the wildest or, as one of Mr. Darwin's own illustrations allows us to add, the most murderous revolutions. At a moment when every artificial principle of authority seems undermined, we have no other guarantee for the order and peace of life, except in the eternal authority of those elementary principles of duty which are independent at all times and all circumstances. There is much reason to fear that loose philosophy, stimulated by an irrational religion, has done not a little to weaken the force of these principles in France, and that this is, at all events, one potent element in the disorganisation of French society. A man incurs a grave responsibility who, with the authority of a well-earned reputation, advances at such a time the disintegrating speculations of this book. He ought to be capable of supporting them by the most conclusive evidence of facts. To put them forward on such incomplete evidence, such cursory investigation, such hypothetical arguments, is more than *unscientific*—it is *reckless.*"

THE WRITINGS

OF

THOMAS CARLYLE.

"Hooded and wrapped about with that strange and antique garb, there walks a kingly, a most royal soul, even as the Emperor Charles walked, amidst solemn cloisters under a monk's cowl—a monarch still in soul."—*Longfellow.*

THE WRITINGS OF THOMAS CARLYLE.

PERHAPS there is not to be found in the whole range of English literature a greater literary phenomenon than the subject of our present study, Thomas Carlyle. In the peculiar constitution of his mind there are many seeming heterogeneous elements which give to him as a writer, if not originality, yet a marked individuality, distinguishing him from all others. In him there is all the earnest, practical energy characteristic of the objective mind of the Scotch, combined with the vivid imagination and deep subjective mind of the German. His ideas are expressed in language wild, grotesque, and sometimes terrible, such as men may long remember; in fact, our language does not give full play to the singular freaks of his wild fancy. In it he is "cabined, cribbed, confined," and anon he breaks through into sentences half German, half English, mingled with slang, street cries, and words which cannot be found in either ancient or modern lexicons, yet relieved here and there by bursts of eloquence as grand and impressive as can be found in our literature. A rabble of unknown authors, unheard-of editors and correspondents, start up in nearly every page, lay siege to your understanding, and play off all manner of quaint pranks of rhetorical manœuvre. Unverifiable quotations from Teufelsdröckh, Herr Sauerteig, M'Crowdy, Crabbe, and Co., the Houndsditch editor, Jefferson Brick the Yankee, and a host of others, are pitted against you in the rear and the flank, while hard and unpronounceable words are knocked against your brains in order to compel your judgment to surrender. These are the means our author uses to go round and through his subject, and to present it in all its possible lights. Nothing is too high or too low, and all human life is interesting to him, whether in the pages of the Newgate Calendar or the Book of Martyrs.

It has been well said that "unprepared readers, coming for the first time upon the writings of Thomas Carlyle, are apt enough to be confounded and repelled. It is like finding one's self alone on a desolate road, with a big, suspicious-looking, bludgeon-armed fellow-traveller; now, you fancy he is about to strike you, now, to leave you when you really need his help. At one moment he is talking with the most unequivocally sardonic scorn, of some institution, or function, or thought, you have been taught to hallow; at another he is squelching the very brains out of some poor devilkin who has tried to insult the said institution, function, or thought, in some other fashion than his. Then, he will appeal to you, to all that is manly and godly in you, to give your assent to some quite old-world truth which you never knew yourself doubting; then he will seriously ask you, whether you suppose things are going on in and around you as they ought. Anon, he has broken away from your side, and is crooning-up into the azure depths a lament that would wring tears from the very stones, if they would try to understand it. In the twinkling of an eye he is back upon you, looking at you earnestly, not without fierceness, and over your inmost soul rolling surge after surge of most terrific prophecy, with applications in every paragraph to yourself. A word here and there seems to come out of the very page and spit upon you—another word, a whole page of words, to flash light down into the deepest parts of the soul."

Carlyle's style is certainly a stumbling-block to critics, and many a thoughtful reader is repelled from the study of his writings by language which often transcends the bounds of intelligibleness, and which brings nothing but confusion and contradiction to his mind. This corruption of language would almost argue some grave defect in the constitution of his mind; as a rough boss or excrescence upon a noble tree is not only a deformity, but it is an indication of unsoundness also. Language, it is well said, is part of man's character; and there is a physiognomy of the speech, as well as of the face, in individuals and in nations. Truly, indeed, says the poet: "We must be free or die who speak the tongue that Shakespeare spake." The English language is not to be equalled for its natural purity, simplicity, and majesty. That language now girdles the earth, and we should be false to our Saxon blood if we did not endeavour to keep "the melody of our sweet isle" free from degradation and corruption.

Yet, despite these eccentricities of thought and manner, the man who has wielded influence over some of the leading minds of the age, such as Mill, Ruskin, Tyndall,

Emerson, Dickens, and others, who have avowed their deep obligations to him, and who represent nearly every shade of opinion, must be acknowledged as a rare genius. In an address to students, Professor Tyndall says: "I must ever remember with gratitude that through three long cold German winters Carlyle placed me in my tub, even when ice was on its surface, at five o'clock every morning, not slavishly, but cheerfully, meeting each day's studies with a resolute will, determined whether victor or vanquished, not to shrink from difficulty. I never should have gone through Analytical Geometry and the Calculus had it not been for those men (Carlyle and Emerson). I never should have become a physical investigator, and hence without them I should not have been here to-day." J. S. Mill says "That the good Carlyle's writings did him was not as philosophy to instruct, but as poetry to animate." To Carlyle, Dickens, after years of acquaintance paid the homage of hero worship when he said, "I would at all times go further to see Carlyle than any man alive."

One of the chief causes of Carlyle's influence arises undoubtedly from his sincere and firm conviction of the truth he utters. His soul is full of earnestness, and nearly every line of his writings bears the strong impress of his spirit, and the stamp of "I believe" upon it. A reverence and faith in that which is true, a deep hatred of that which is false, a belief in the eternal and immutable laws of God in the world, in the sovereign right of duty, in the dignity and solemnity of human life—these are the articles of his faith, which he ever proclaims with new and impressive earnestness. In words which, like Luther's, "are half battles," that fly off sometimes in fiery sentences, like sparks from his fierce glowing soul, as he utters his indignant protest against human wrong and misery, against cant and falsehood and the vices and crimes which dishonour human nature, or again utters his prophetic warnings and denunciations, after the manner of the old Hebrew seers.

He has roused men from that sleep of indifference and security into which they had been lulled by the Utilitarian philosophy of Bentham, the cool scepticism of the *Edinburgh Review*, since supplemented by the mechanical philosophy of Mill, and the anthropological speculations of Darwin. The outcome of their teaching was to regard all religions alike as superstitions; the great problems of man's life and destiny as insolvable, and, therefore, best left alone; morality as a set of rules based upon political economy; parliament, an earthly providence, which by wise laws was to shower down the greatest amount of happiness upon the greatest number. "For our happiness was dependent upon external circumstances; nay, the strength and dignity of the mind within us was itself the creature and consequence of these." Science was to take the place of religion, and to regenerate the world without faith or worship. Man was a calculating machine, and to calculate well was wisdom. Virtue and sugar-plums formed the theory of life. The act from which the greatest amount of pleasure could be obtained was virtuous, and that which produced the most pain was vice. This dry, barren, and godless creed was the very reverse of Carlyle's, and he has uttered fury, scorn, and denunciation, with withering and blasting invective against it. He has taught us, that there are other powers than Acts of Parliament for the amelioration of our race; forces, beside steam and electricity, to shape and mould our being; that there is a higher sphere of activity and duty than our work in the material world; that virtue consists in the sacrifice and not the enjoyment of self; that the end of existence is not the fullest enjoyment of the sensuous attributes, but in the complete development of the highest faculties of the moral and spiritual nature; that happiness depends on the mind within, and not in the circumstances which are without. For truly, says the poet, "Where is the beauty, love and truth we seek but in our minds?"

In combating the Utilitarian's theory of life, he says: "If what thou namest Happiness be our true aim, then are we all astray. With stupidity and sound digestion man may front much. But what, in these dull, unimaginative days, are the terrors of Conscience to the diseases of the Liver! Not on Morality, but on Cookery, let us build our stronghold; there brandishing our frying-pan, as censer, let us offer sweet incense to the Devil, and live at ease on the fat things *he* has provided for his Elect!"*

This materialistic and mechanical philosophy, which scornfully rejected every standard of value but what affected the outward man, was to Carlyle the greatest evil of our age: like Aaron's rod it swallowed up all others. To him its system was wrong from its very basis; it commenced the problem of life at the wrong end, and endeavoured to poise the pyramid on its apex. "The past experience of ages, and the universal assent of mankind," were set aside, and the consequence was that it

---

* *Sartor Resartus.*

turned our History, Philosophy, and Religion all topsy-turvy. In its history God appears nowhere, for men were the sole actors; its philosophy explained all the mysteries of the universe; yea, the boundless universe itself was regarded as "a lifeless machine, a huge body without soul, floating over the abyss of annihilation between chance and fatality."

Mr. Mill's later speculations, published since his death, may be taken as the *ultimatum* of this philosophy, and it is well that we can see the end thereof. The words of Richter, once applied by Carlyle to Diderot, are as true of Mill: "The unhappy man had sailed through the Universe of Worlds and found no Maker thereof; had descended to the abysses where Being no longer casts its shadow, and felt only the rain drops trickle down; and seen only the gleaming rainbow of Creation, which originated from no Sun; and heard only the everlasting storm which no one governs; and looked upwards for the Divine Eye, and beheld only the black, bottomless, glaring Death's Eye-socket; such, with all his wide voyagings, was the philosophic fortune he had realised."

It is against this Atheistic philosophy Carlyle has lifted up his warning voice, and, with terrible earnestness, like soul speaking to soul, has he endeavoured to bring back the minds of men to the existence of a God-ruled and miraculous world, and to teach them that the laws of Nature are not like dead machinery, but that they are the ever-living operations of the Lord of Nature. This voice, like the lonely wail of a prophet, breaking in as it did upon our egotistical 19th century, to many seemed new and strange, as it uttered its warnings of "woe, woe" upon our backsliding nation. The 19th century had reached the highest point of optimism and egotism, and its ears had been deafened by the pœans which had been sung on "the Progress of the Species," "the March of Civilization" and "the Decay of Superstition." Men stared at each other with large eyes of fear and astonishment as Carlyle revealed the hidden workings of disease in our social and political system. Can these things be, said they, or is it the result of morbid rancour and misanthropy? But voices were heard from the teeming streets, the tiring factories; from the typhus-haunted and sorrow-stricken lanes and alleys cf our large towns answering, "It is even so: this man speaks truly."

Carlyle's hatred of the false is but an inversion of his love for the true. No man has bared his head with greater reverence in acknowledgment of a Supreme and Infinite Being, or looked up to the heavens in silent self-communion (though he has declared it a "sad sight") "at that host of white-robed pilgrims that travel along the vault of the nightly sky." No man has more earnestly sought to decipher those hieroglyphics traced by that unseen finger upon the universe, whose Author and Writer is God; or to understand His freshly-uttered word as He speaks through the souls of the greatest and noblest of the sons of men; for one of the articles of Carlyle's creed is, "that God does speak through men to the generation;" and, also, "that the highest Being reveals Himself in man." Well said St. Chrysostom, with his lips of gold, "the true Shekinah is man." Where else is the God's presence manifested, not to our eyes only, but to our hearts, as in our fellow man? Carlyle is never tired of quoting a favourite passage from Novalis: "There is but one temple in the universe, and that is the Body of Man; nothing is holier than that high form. Bending before men is a reverence done to this revelation in the flesh. We touch heaven when we lay our hand on a human body." "This sounds," says Carlyle, "much like a mere flourish of rhetoric, but it is not so. If well meditated, it will turn out to be a scientific fact; the expression in such words as can be had of the actual truth of the thing. We are the miracle of miracles —the great, inscrutible mystery of God. We cannot understand it; we know not how to speak of it, but we may feel and know, if we like, that it is verily so." But, alas! Carlyle has to tell us that there is a devil dwelling in man as well as a divinity, and that one of the greatest allies of the Prince of Darkness is ignorance. Venerable to him is the hard hand, the rugged face all weather-tanned, beaming with its rude intelligence; for it is the face of a man living man-like. "But how often," he says, " while the body stands so broad and brawny the soul lies blinded, dwarfed, stupefied, almost annihilated, for the want of knowledge." So that the man is too often but like a patent digester of so much animal and vegetable food; whose thoughts never soar higher than a hot dinner on Sundays, or a pipe and pot in the tap-room at night. One could verily weep at such pictures of stagnant power, undeveloped excellence, imbruted virtue, and stifled genius. "That one man should die ignorant, who had capacity for knowledge," this he calls, " a tragedy; but what," he adds, " if it were to happen more than twenty times in the minute, as by some computations it does."

In Carlyle's wit and humour there are many peculiar

characteristics. His wit is of a heavy, thumping kind, like the battering ram of old, hammering away with "thunderlike percussion" at some old abuse or time-worn institution. He reminds us of the heathen tradition of one of the gods, who is described as "all hands, all eyes, all feet," to seek out, overtake, and punish falsehood and wrong. His humour is often of such a kind as makes us laugh through tears, and which laughs itself in its most savage moods. It has in it a wild, grim fancy, with something of the fierce, grotesque, and fiery earnestness of Hogarth, with the free, daring caricature of Cruikshank. A rough, rugged, vehement spirit is in him, as well as a hearty humour, which ever and anon breaks out, sporting with the foibles, fancies, and manners of our age. Many a hearty laugh has he given us at John Bull's expense as he views, with a half-serious, half-comic eye, his stone and lime Church, his time-worn institutions, his glorious constitution and Charter, his direct railroad understanding. Yet we feel, despite Bull's anomalies and failings, and perhaps because of them, we cannot choose but to love him the more.

In studying this strange genius it will be impossible in so brief a notice to consider his relations to each of the various departments of literature which he has contributed, as an essayist, translator, biographer, historian, and politician. In glancing at his principal writings, we hope to treat them in a catholic spirit, to give, as far as we are able, a fair summary of them, and at the same time endeavour to put his teachings into some practical shape, so that we may learn what his mission to this age has been.

One of the first works which brought Carlyle into notice was his admirable *Life of Schiller*, which appeared in the *London Magazine* in the year 1823. This was afterwards published in a separate form, and translated into German, with a preface, by Goethe. Its style is free from that rugged phraseology, for which its author is now so often condemned. Although there is displayed in this work great depth of thought, as well as a keen insight into the German mind and character, and, moreover, that sympathetic charm which is so essential to a good biography, its success was not so great as it deserved.

In the year 1824 appeared the *Translation of Wilhelm Meister*," a novel from the German of Goethe, which has been called " the greatest work of the greatest German writer." Whatever opinions may be held with regard to the practical aim and tendency of the book, this translation into English must be regarded as a masterpiece of literary transposition. This translation provoked the celebrated attack upon Goethe by Jeffrey in the *Edinburgh Review*. But the critic used this book more as an opportunity to make a fierce onslaught on the Germans and their literature than as a criticism upon the author's work, which he would not or did not care to understand. This novel, we think, shows all the strength and weakness of Goethe's genius. Throughout there is very little action, and no plot. Wilhelm Meister is a sort of milk-and-water hero, who in his apprenticeship-travels meets with a series of adventures, and is by turns either the slave of woman or of circumstances. He joins a company of strolling players, and his ideal notions of the drama painfully contrast with the realities of an actor's life, for his companions, male and female, have scarcely a rag of virtue among them. Although in the novel there are no perfect forms of individual life, yet there is shown a profound insight into human character. We are more interested in the conversations and reflections, in the knowledge of men and nature conveyed through the characters, than in the characters themselves. This novel was written, according to its author, for no moral or immoral purpose, without any express tendency. "The whole work seems to say nothing more than that man, despite all his follies and errors, being led by a higher hand, reaches some happy goal at last." A want of cohesion may account for some of its apparent contradictions, there is a strange mixture of vulgar sensuality and noble sentiments: the shrewdest practical wisdom with the loftiest idealism, and the happiest humour with the keenest sarcasm. But for the English mind its greatest beauties will never redeem its great blemishes. It is difficult to understand Carlyle's admiration, next to worship, of Goethe, unless it is upon the principle of sympathy of the like with the unlike. In Goethe's cold, clear, majestic intellect there was an Alp-like sublimity which raised itself above all sympathy with the actions of this working-day world. His philosophy seems to be cold, selfish, and egotistical—a renovation of the old Pagan worship, with its worldly maxims. He condescended to patronize Christianity; but there is no trace in his life of his ever, in a Christian sense, worshipping its Author. It seems strange that two spirits so wide apart and with such great differences should yet be akin—one reminding us of a colossal iceberg, the other of a huge, flaming volcano.

After the translation of *Wilhelm Meister*, Carlyle contributed to some of the first-class magazines of the day, where are to be found those inimitable articles which were afterwards published in four volumes under the head of *Miscellaneous Essays*. Those who have read the graphic sketches of Burns, Richter, Goethe, Johnson, and others will acknowledge the wondrous power or sympathetic faculty by which the writer is enabled to identify himself with the thoughts and emotions, the passions and pursuits of these great men, thereby bringing their human nature to our own level, and giving us a charm almost approaching friendship for them. These portraits may be considered as the happiest results of his pen; they are the work of a true artist, presenting to us not ideal representations, but characters of flesh and blood. One characteristic passage we quote from his article on *Burns:* "The excellence of Burns is, indeed, among the rarest, whether in poetry or prose, but, at the same time, it is plain and easily recognised; his *sincerity*, his indisputable air of truth. Here are no fabulous woes or joys; no hollow fantastic sentimentalities, no wire-drawn refinings, either in thought or feeling: the passion that is traced before us has glowed in a living heart; the opinion he utters has risen in his own understanding, and had been a light to his own steps. He does not write from hearsay, but from sight and experience; it is the scenes that he has lived and laboured amidst that he describes: those scenes, rude and humble as they are, have kindled beautiful emotions in his soul, noble thoughts, and definite resolves;

and he speaks forth what is in him, not from any outward call of vanity or interest, but because his heart is too full to be silent. He speaks it with such melody and modulation as he can, 'in homely rustic jingle,' but it is his own, and genuine. This is the grand secret for finding readers and retaining them: let him who would move and convince others, be first moved and convinced himself."

About the same time as the *Miscellaneous Essays*, was written, what has been called by many of Carlyle's admirers his best work, *Sartor Resartus* (*The Tailor Done Over*, the name of an old Scotch ballad); *or, The Life and Opinions of Herr Teufelsdrockh* (Devil's Dust). This book professes to be an autobiography, of which Carlyle assumes the character of Editor, but there is no doubt that through Teufelsdröckh he has told us something of his own life and opinions, and, moreover, given us a significant portrait of himself. An unprepared reader, taking up this book, would most likely be repelled by its strange sentences and uncouth terminology. Of his sentences, the assumed Editor says: "Perhaps not more than nine-tenths stand straight on their legs; the remainder are in quite angular attitudes, buttressed up by props (of parentheses and dashes), a few even sprawl-out helplessly on all sides, quite broken-backed and dismembered." But what would astonish the reader more would be that strange dissertation upon "Clothes," which forms the opening chapters in the volume. Gentlemen of the smooth-kid school will find themselves wofully disappointed if they search this book for instructions in tying the cravat, or to study the latest fashion. The philosophy of clothes comprehends the philosophy of things in general. These clothes are the garments of the invisible, which the spirit of nature is ever weaving "at Time's loud-roaring loom." They are the forms, modes, or vestures by which the ever-living thought of the world evolves in institutions, forms of philosophy, and religion. These forms are ever changing, "they wax old as doth a garment;" but the spirit that produces them is immortal. Institutions fade and crumble into dust, and "these decays but foster new creations." Destruction and creation, death and birth go on together. Being is ever a birth into a higher being; for "the great world-secret is growth." It is written, "the heavens and the earth shall fade away like a vesture, which indeed they are; the time-vesture of the Eternal. Whatsoever sensibly exists, whatsoever represents Spirit to Spirit, is properly a clothing, a suit of raiment put on for a season and to be laid off. Thus, in this one pregnant subject of clothes, rightly understood, is included all that men have thought, dreamed, done, and been; the whole external universe, and what it holds, is but clothing; and the essence of all science lies in the Philosophy of Clothes."

Carlyle teaches us in this quaint way to look through the shows or vestures of things into things themselves, and to put aside as a worn-out garment that which had once the form of life (like the cast skin of a serpent), but which is now dead, since men, by clinging with superstitious awe to those forms and traditions from which the truth has died out, become the slaves of shams and delusions.

We have in this book a real and not an imaginary life. It is the true biography of a man of thought struggling for life and light; the life procession of a soul following after truth. It endeavours to trace the efforts of the human mind in this long and arduous struggle; to reveal its hopes and fears; its long years of patient watching; its moments of despair and hours of triumph. It is a life drama, with scenes of intense colouring, thoughts at times burning and vivid, at others dim, meteoric and distant, beckoning us like ghosts into the viewless regions of the silent spiritland. Over all these changes there hovers a wild spirit of poetry, attuning the music of our feelings through all the wide ranging sympathies of our nature: now wailing forth the soft hymn of devotion, or trembling with the agitation and storm of the choral passion; now "savage and shrill," like the wild notes of the pibroch, that coil up the courage and fury of the soul, or again piping the joyous music of a marriage festival; yet there are discords, dissonances, and plaintive notes, that make the heart in love with woe.

To that poor, languishing, time-killing reader, who gives other people the trouble of thinking for him, this book will be useless. To him whose faith is a dead creed, whose soul is comfortably settled in the ready furnished lodgings of tradition, this book will be of little value. But to him who has battled with doubts which, like giants, huge and blatant, have risen up before his soul, threatening it with annihilation, who, like Teufelsdröckh, has felt himself a wanderer in a forsaken and fatherless world, and by his self-will has defied it, and sought to trample it with its injuries under his feet, as the old Greek philosopher Zeno and our modern Byron did—but who has emerged from this "Everlasting No" to the "Everlasting Yea" (as Carlyle describes it)—self-annihilation, and not self-gratification is the desideratum of his life, teaching him to "love the World while it injures him, and even because it injures him, as a greater than Zeno did whom the World needed and who was sent,"—to such this book will be—

> "More precious far
> Than that accumulated store of Gold,
> And Orient Gems, which, for a day of need,
> The Sultan hides within ancestral tombs."

Yet we think there are other defects in the book, besides its harsh jagged sentences and repulsive style, "with the startling whirl of incongruous juxtaposition, which, of a truth, must to many readers seem as amazing as if the Pythia on the tripod should have struck up a drinking song, or Thersites had caught the prophetic strain of Cassandra." In Teufelodröckh there is much that is great and good, but he is a solitary dreamer, and lives in a world of speculation instead of action. Therefore his good thoughts are not much better than good dreams; he seems to waste himself by consuming internally his strong emotions of pity and love. His philosophy smells strongly of the midnight oil and tobacco-smoke. As an isolated being he lacks that genial sympathy which bathes everything in the sunlight of its love, prompting men to co-operate with their fellows, to join hand, as well as heart, in endeavouring to perfect our common humanity. His thoughts are too irregular, and not formed into a proper series and sequence, they are too suggestive, leading us into a region of conjectures, and we are bewildered in a labyrinth of guesses; for though he has heaps of opinions he has but few convictions. Yet there is a Titanic energy wrestling with and conquering doubt and despondency, tossing about huge fragments of thought, and upheaving the inner nature of the man.

In the year 1840 Carlyle delivered before a select London audience his *Lectures on Heroes, Hero-Worship, and The Heroic in History*. These lectures embody one of his great articles of faith, the gist of which has now become quite a proverb amongst us, viz.—" that the hour and the man are born together,"—" that universal history, the history of what man has accomplished in this world, is at bottom the history of the great men who have worked here." The great drama of life, as it evolves in the form of history, shows us comparatively few men in each generation. Each age in the history of the world is a great man's epoch. Paganism had its Odin in which the hero was Deity—Mahometanism its Mahomet, in which the hero was Prophet. The grand old days of chivalry had also its hero poet in Shakespeare, and the Christian Church in Dante. Out of a fast-sinking and decaying Church arose Luther and Knox as heroic priests. The Reformation had its stern Puritan King in Cromwell, "Even Democracy itself, the ostensible denial of all worship, found its soldier in Napoleon, and worshipped him." These men were God's ministers, the instruments by which he worked His will in the world, sometimes to exalt and sometimes to cast down and punish nations. Universal history is to Carlyle a Bible, "which every born man, till once the soul and eyesight are extinguished in him, can, and must, with his own eyes, see the God's finger-writing." The history of England is the record of the divine appearances among us. "Beyond doubt," he says, "the Almighty Maker made this England, too, and has been, and for ever is, miraculously present here, divinely avenging and divinely saving and rewarding." With this faith Carlyle looks through the past, and has hope in the present and future, for God never fails through His instruments. These lectures on *Hero Worship* give us the key for reading and understanding what we consider Carlyle's greatest work, *The History of the French Revolution*. Mr. Mill was one of the first to hail this book "as one of those productions of genius which are above all rules and are a law to themselves." When the MS. of the first volume was finished it was lent to a friend, and unfortunately, by some accident, burnt, and its author had to go through the great task of re-writing it. This book is the most difficult of all his works to criticise, or we might say that it is "criticism proof." Its style flashes with the fire of the subject. It is abrupt, rugged, and meteoric, full of colossal thoughts and images, beautiful, artistic descriptions, vivid and lifelike sketches, with deep and subtle analyses of the human mind and character. Throughout there is a strange barbaric splendour, an accumulation of fantastic and sometimes fearful images, a chaotic wildness which seems, perhaps, more suggestive of the might and fury of the tempest than of the overpowering strength of light. It is an unrhymed poem, a modern Iliad, the burden of a nation's woes and sorrows, when writhing under the retribution of God. We look with wondrous eye into that Sea of Terrors, agitated and lashed by the stormy winds of passion, the mighty waves foaming and madly dashing as from the "bosom of deep hell," each wave as it were a human countenance, "imploring, wrathful, and despairing," with a look never to be forgotten. Mirabeau rises up "in fiery, rough figure, with black Samson locks under the slouch hat, a carbuncled, grim, pitted visage, like a tiger that had had the small-pox—a man of instincts and insights, a man nevertheless who will glare fiercely on any object, and see through it, and conquer it; for he has intellect, he has will, force beyond other men—a man, not with *logic-spectacles*, but with an *eye*." "That greenish-coloured individual is an advocate of Arras, his name is Maximilian Robespierre. A long-winded, incorruptible man whose eloquence was acrid, implacable, impotent, dull, drawling, barren as the Harmattan wind." "Jean Paul Marat looks forth through a bleared, dull, acrid, woe-stricken face, redolent of soot and horse drugs. The lone Stylites who was hurled down suddenly from his pillar—*whitherward* He who made him knows.*"* "That huge, brawny figure, through whose black brows and rude, flattened face there looks a waste energy as of Hercules not yet furibund." Follow him, and as you see him stand ranked at the bar of Tinville you tremble as he gives his address: "My name is Danton," a name tolerably known in the Revolution, "my abode will soon be Annihilation, but I shall live in the Pantheon of History." We see him again as he carries a high look in the death-cart, and at the foot of the scaffold he is heard to ejaculate, "O, my wife, my well beloved, I shall never see thee more then," but, interrupting himself, "Danton, no weakness," so he passes away to his unknown home. "He with the long curling locks, with the face of dingy blackguardism, wondrously irradiated with genius, as if a naptha-lamp burnt within it, that figure is Camille Desmoulins, a fellow of infinite shrewdness, wit, nay humour, one of the sprightliest, clearest souls in all these millions." Poor Louis was more fit for a tradesman than a king. He, the descendant of a long line of monarchs, looks one of the least heroic of all the victims, as he stands on the edge of the scaffold speaking in dumb show, his face very red; with desperate struggles the executioners bind him to their plank. "Abbé Edgeworth stooping, bespeaks him 'Son of Saint Louis, ascend to heaven.' The axe clanks down; and a king's life is shorn away."

All these and many more rise up and are engulphed in this sea of blood and fire. The air is lurid and thick with dread and awful shapes, for there are—

> "Strange screams of death,
> And prophesying with accents terrible,
> Of dire combustion and confused events,
> New hatched to the woful time."

Whoever has studied this book will understand the aim and object of the writer. It is a practical commentary upon the inspired text, "The nation that will not serve God shall perish," with wondrous power. Carlyle has described old France rushing down, sweeping away all forms of royalty, government, and religion, giving way before a young France, who has found a new gospel for the regeneration of mankind. The gospel, according to Jean Jacques Rousseau, which proclaimed a universal millenium at hand, vaunting liberty, equality, and fraternity, general peace and happiness for all men, but which, alas! proved instead a gospel of anarchy, scepticism, and sensualism, bringing a reign of error, cruelty, and bloodshed upon the land. This people sowed the wind, and had to reap the whirlwind. So many centuries had been adding together, century transmitting it with increase to century, the sum of wickedness, of falsehood, oppression of man by man. Kings were sinners and priests were, and the people. Everything before the Revolution was hollow and false. Belief and loyalty had passed away, and only the cant and echo of them remained. All solemnity had become pageantry, and the nobles had become little more than ornamental figures, who thought of nothing more than dressing gracefully and eating sumptuously, while the nation was bankrupt and the people starving. These things could not remain unless that God's universe was Belial's and a lie. The cry of the wretched, starved millions went up before Heaven, and the answer did come in a horror of great darkness, and shakings of the world, and a cup of trembling, which the nations had to drink, "and the anger of the Lord did kindle against them . . . and their carcasses were torn in the midst of the streets." The object of this book is to prove that there is law and justice in this world; that there is an Eternal centre of right and truth; that nothing but what emanates from that centre hath a natural right to live; that although judgment for an unjust thing is sternly delayed, and men and nations perish as without law, yet that judgment will come, shaking, tearing up, and trampling upon everything that is not planted in Truth and Righteousness; that all forms of tyranny live but in variety of disease; "that blood begets blood, injustice breeds injustice; that curses and falsehoods do verily return always home." Here an innocent king had to bear the sins of many generations, especially those of his miserable predecessor, Louis XV. Yet this martyr's death was infinitely preferable to that of the vile sinner who spent his last days in his foul harem, "a mass of abhorred clay," forsaken by his harlots, yet surrounded by priests chaunting their "Prayers of Forty Hours." "He," as the Abbé Georgel records, "made the *amende honourable* to God, had a true repentance of three days' standing, and so fell asleep in the Lord." "Asleep in the Lord!" adds Carlyle in bitter comment. "If such a mass of laziness and lust fell asleep in the Lord, who is it that falls asleep elsewhere?"

What strikes the reader is the terrible earnestness of the writer. This burns in every page in its talismanic words, its thrilling apostrophes, its vivid lightning thoughts, its long-drawn thunder peals of eloquence, its wild, savage, yet mournful humour, its flaming yet ghastly pictures—

"With hues as when some painter dips
His pen in dyes of earthquake and eclipse."

These various elements confused, commingled, and mutually inflamed, make this history a fiery beacon, a warning for our age, for which purpose Carlyle has written it. In his book, *Past and Present*, he has described this French Revolution as "The cruelest portent that has risen into created space these ten centuries; let us hail it with awe-struck repentant hearts; as the voice once more of a God, though of one in wrath."

We do not think that this history will ever be a popular

one. It is more a prose poem than a history; more a series of magnificently varying panoramic pictures than an index and record of events. It is like reading history by a rapid succession of flashes, and the mind often tires at the repeated shocks of surprise, and is dazzled by the incessant coruscations. It lacks the precise form, general detail, and chronological arrangement, to make it an English reading book; for, as Sydney Smith somewhere humorously remarks, "The English are a calm, reflecting nation; they love dates, names, and certificates. In the midst of the most heart-rending narration, Bull enquires the day of the month, the year of our Lord, the name of the parish, and the countersign of three or four respectable householders."

The lesson that we read from this strange history may be summed up in these lines of Frederick Von Logau, translated by Longfellow :—

"Though the mills of God grind slowly, yet they grind exceeding small;
Though with patience He stands waiting, with exactness grinds He all."

Carlyle's next works were *Chartism* and *Past and Present*. In these books he grapples with some of the social and political problems of the day. Our shams, dead creeds and hollow formulas are his nightmare, and we think sometimes his endeavours to free himself and the world from them are like the fitful ineffectual struggles peculiar to that morbid state. He seems to lose himself in his wanderings through what he calls "the pestiferous mists and quagmires of our age." He warns us of an approaching deluge which threatens to overwhelm us in destruction, and although he is a "preacher of righteousness," yet he constructs no ark for our safety and refuge, and with ruthless irony and sarcasm he overturns the little logical lifeboats which have been set afloat by the Utilitarians, Philosophical Radicals, and others. He flings contemptuous epithets at every institution, whether moral, religious, social, or political; gives the name of "Beaver Science" to the studies and generalizations of our modern scientists, "Logic Choppers" to the metaphysicians of the 18th and 19th centuries, who, after reasoning themselves out of their five senses, can no further go. The external and mechanical forms of religion he calls the religion of the "rotatory Calabash," referring to the written prayers which the Kalmucks put into a revolving Calabash, and which, turned by the wind, produces, it is supposed, perpetual adoration. Political Economists are called "Professors of the dismal Science." Philosophical Theorists are "Word mongers," and to be compared to "Spinning Dervishes," who with "swift twirling motion make no progress, but end where they begin." On every institution he writes "Lies, Lies, Lies!" "There is nothing," says an eminent Frenchman, "he does not tread down and ravage. The symmetrical constructions of human art and thought, dispersed and upset, are piled under his hands into a vast mass of shapeless ruins, from the top of which he gesticulates and fights like a conquering savage." In *Past and Present* he has represented the ancient and the modern worker. In the character of an Ancient Monk he has described one of his Heroes, a worker of the past, Abbot Samson, a man of vigorous thought, word, and action, who has been taught to govern because he has learned to obey, elected to be Abbot over the Convent of St. Edmondsbury. He finds it, from the neglect of his predecessors, half bankrupt, the monks insubordinate, greedy, and quarrelsome, of drunken and dissolute habits. Through Abbot Samson and his wise Government, Carlyle has sketched his Utopia, and endeavoured to work out the great problem of governing Nations. We read how on all sides the Abbot laid about him like a man,— of the radical reform of his economics, how he struggled unweariedly to arrange and place on some intelligible footing the affairs and dues of his dominion,— of that terrible flash of anger which awed the discontented and lazy monks, of his courts, where neither gold nor silver could help a man to confound his enemy. Everywhere we see this missionary of order declaring war against disorder and ruin, and like a true soldier regarding neither his days without rest, his nights without sleep, nor even his life that he may do the duty set before him. Here we have some beautiful glimpses into the monastic times of Old England, some seven centuries ago, through the authentic chronicle of Jocelin of Brakelond, a certain old St. Edmondsbury Monk, who has left a contemporary record of the doings of those times. Carlyle has used these materials, and, with the ardour of his poetic soul, infused new life into them, so that the past seems leafy and blossoming again, and is brought up before our imagination fresh as the beauty of Spring, yet, excepting the few glimpses which Jocelin has given us in his chronicle, we cannot but feel that the whole is a fine romance, "a Past that never had a Present," and that Carlyle has reflected and reproduced in an imaginative form his own thoughts and convictions. The ancient Monk, the worker of the past, is contrasted with the worker of the present, and terrible are Carlyle's warnings and denunciations of our age. He has quite reversed Pope's motto, for with him, Whatever is, is wrong. We have all eaten the fruit of the tree of lies. We "have forgotten God, have quietly closed our eyes to the eternal substance of things, and opened them only to the shows and shams of things. We quietly believe this Universe to be intrinsically a great unintelligible Perhaps; extrinsically, clear enough, it is a great, most extensive Cattlefold and Workhouse, with most extensive kitchen-ranges, dining-tables—whereat he is wise who can find a place! All the Truth of this Universe is uncertain; only the profit and loss of it, the pudding and praise of it, are and remain very visible to the practical man."

Our Chancery and certain other Law Courts are but chimneys for the devilry and contention of men to escape by. Our governors consist not in able men, but in men able to get appointed. The chief aim of government is declared to be the greatest happiness of the greatest number, which generally means that the greatest number is number one; and the people are seeking for some Morrison's Pill Act of Parliament or remedial measure which they could swallow, one good time, and then go on in their old courses, cleared from all miseries and mischiefs. Such, then, is his estimate of our age, an age which boasts itself in its civilization, in the march of intellect, and in the travels of the schoolmaster. We would ask Carlyle if there were no quackeries or shams two or three centuries ago, if there is not written against them a terrible record of priestcraft, witchcraft, superstition, outrage, and crime; if the Smithfield burnings are extinguished in his memory, and if Bunyan had not, even in the Puritan age, as many significant names for cant and hypocrisy as he has? Then why does he place our age so far below all others? In reading this book one is reminded of Macaulay's saying "that from childhood he had heard of nothing but decay, and seen nothing but progress." The world, no doubt, is a great deal better and a great deal worse than we know it to be. Every age has its marked characteristics, its good and evil tendencies, and while the good is quiet and unobtrusive the evil is seen and remembered by its very repulsiveness. In *Past and Present*, Carlyle proclaims "The Gospel of Labour," *Laborare est Orare*—"Work is Worship." What is thy work? he asks, and the answer is the test of the man's truth and nobility, for work is the spiritual revelation of the man, doubt of any sort cannot be removed except by action, for there is a perennial nobleness, and even sacredness in work. Were he never so benighted, forgetful of his high calling, there is always hope in a man that actually and earnestly works. In idleness alone is there perpetual despair. Consider how, even in the meanest sorts of labour, the whole soul of a man is composed into a kind of real harmony the instant he sets himself to work. Doubt, desire, sorrow, remorse, indignation, despair itself, all these, like hell-dogs, lie beleaguering the soul of the poor day-worker, as of every man, but he bends himself with free valour against his task, and all these are stilled, all these shrink murmuring far off into their caves. The man is now a man. One characteristic extract we will make from this book, which is a modern application of an ancient fable. " Perhaps few narratives in history or mythology are more significant than that Moslem one, of Moses and the dwellers by the Dead Sea. A tribe of men dwelt on the shores of that same asphaltic lake, and having forgotten, as we are all too prone to do, the inner facts of nature, and taken up with the falsities and outer semblances of it, were fallen into sad conditions—verging indeed towards a certain far deeper lake. Whereupon it pleased kind Heaven to send them the prophet Moses with an instructive word of warning, out of which might have sprung 'remedial measures' not a few. But no; the men of the Dead Sea discovered, as the valet-species always does in heroes or prophets, no comeliness in Moses; listened with real tedium to Moses, with light grinning or with splenetic sniffs and sneers, affecting even to yawn, and signified, in short, that they found him a humbug and even a bore. Such was the candid theory these men of the Asphalte Lake formed to themselves of Moses; that probably he was a humbug, that certainly he was a bore."

Moses withdrew: but Nature, and her rigorous veracities, did not withdraw. The men of the Dead Sea, when we next went to visit them, were all changed into Apes;* sitting on the trees there, grinning now in the most un-affected manner; gibbering and chattering very genuine nonsense; finding the whole universe now a most indisputable humbug! The Universe had *become* a Humbug to these apes, who thought it one. There they sit and chatter

---

* Sale's Koran (Introduction).

to this hour: only, I believe, every Sabbath there returns to them a bewildered half-consciousness, half-reminiscence; and they sit, with their wizened, smoke-dried visages, and such an air of supreme tragicality as Apes may; looking out through those blinking, smoke-bleared eyes of theirs into the wonderfulest universal smoky twilight and undecipherable disordered dusk of things; wholly an Uncertainty, Unintelligibility, they and it: and for commentary thereon, here and there an unmusical chatter or mew;—truest, tragicalest humbug conceivable by the mind of man or ape! They made no use of their souls; and so have lost them. Their worship on the Sabbath now is to roost there, with unmusical screeches, and half remember that they had souls. Didst thou never, O traveller, fall-in with parties of this tribe? Meseems they are grown somewhat numerous in our day."

In 1845 appeared Oliver Cromwell's *Letters and Speeches; with Elucidations.* This was one of Carlyle's most elaborate Works. To complete those Letters and Speeches was the labour of years, lightened, no doubt, from the fact of its being a labour of love. Carlyle has not vindicated Cromwell so much as Cromwell has vindicated himself. These letters and speeches quite verify Cromwell's own remarkable prophecy: "I know that God will in His own time vindicate me." His letters, most of them written in the hurry and turmoil of a Campaign, reveal to us a man of large yet tender sympathies; deep religious feelings, mingled with a strong yet simple and childlike faith. They are written in coarse, homely phrase, stamped with the rough energy and sincerity of the man. Those to his family breathe the very spirit of devotional love. They are sincere, for a man is never a hypocrite in his own family. Doubtless Carlyle's devoted attachment to Cromwell has in many cases misled his judgment, so that he has passed over, or treated lightly, some of the great defects and sins of his character. He has so identified himself with his Hero, that at times the Hero and the Editor appear as one. He thinks with his thoughts, sees with his eyes, becomes a Puritan, and realized the Puritan's experience and faith. He has entered into the disputes and controversies of that period; fought over each battle; sat with Cromwell in Parliament; reported and interpolated his speeches, and followed him closer than ever Boswell did his Master, thereby giving us the man as he lived, spoke, and acted. Facts are his data. These he has "walled round with iron-worded proof." For them he laboured for years, seeking among mountains of dusty papers and pamphlets, searching old Registers and Certificates, thus bringing to light many long forgotten things. Every incident he has described with intense pictorial effect. His description of the Hero Oliver going down like a glorious Sun into the Shades of Death, is one of the masterpieces of eloquence in our language.

In 1850 was published the *Latter Day Pamphlets*, wherein Carlyle spoke out again upon the Social disorders of the time,—and this, too, when Optimism was at its high water mark. When soon afterwards under the dome of glass Shem, Ham, and Japheth were shaking hands in token of everlasting peace and eternal brotherhood, as if Paradise lost was soon to be regained; "our dreams and our thoughts were of anything but of fighting, or of the smallest need to fight." Alas! scarcely two years had elapsed before we had drifted into the Crimean War, and were rudely disturbed in our dreams (as we have been many times since) by the tread of innumerable armies, the roaring of cannon, the crossing of bayonets, and the bulletins of the dead and the dying; while our brave army was dwindling away, not by the shot and shell of the enemy, but from hunger, cold and disease, almost in sight of ships in the offing, laden with food, warm clothing, and medical stores, yet unable to discharge their cargoes because nobody could give instructions. Then was it found that Carlyle had not exaggerated the incompetence of our Governing Executive, and a general recognition of the unpalatable truths he had written (for many of his prophecies had become history) was some recompense for the abuse which had been heaped upon him on all sides.

The cool, cruel irony and merciless sarcasm of Swift never steeped his age more in the gall of bitterness than Carlyle has done our own in that cynical Catechism in his pamphlet on Jesuitism, headed, *Pig Philosophy.*

What Carlyle thinks of our *Reform Measures,* &c., may be gathered from one of his later pamphlets called *Shooting Niagara and After.* "All the Milleniums," he says, "I ever heard of heretofore were to be preceded by a 'chaining of the Devil for a thousand years,'—laying *him* up, tied neck and heels, and put beyond stirring, as the preliminary. You, too, have been taking preliminary steps, with more and more ardour, for a thirty years back; but they seem to be all in the opposite direction; a cutting asunder of straps and ties wherever you might find them; pretty indiscriminate of choice in the matter; a general repeal of old regulations, fetters, and restrictions (restrictions on the Devil originally, I believe, for most part, but now fallen slack and ineffectual), which had become unpleasant to many of you,—with loud shouting from the multitude as strap after strap was cut: 'Glory, glory, another strap is gone!'—this, I think, has mainly been the sublime legislative industry of Parliament since it became 'Reform Parliament;' victoriously successful, and thought 'sublime and beneficent by some. So that now hardly any limb of the Devil has a thrum, or tatter of rope or leather left upon it—there needs almost superhuman heroism in you to 'whip' a garotter; no Fenian taken with the reddest hand is to be meddled with, under penalties; hardly a murderer, never so detestable and hideous, but you find him 'insane,' and board him at the public expense." Carlyle tells us that there is as wide a difference between right and wrong as between heaven and hell; that according to the laws of nature wrong doing will bring its punishment, however we by legislation or otherwise may attempt to hinder or avert it. If we do not punish it, it will punish us. This is Law, and the Eternal Laws must be obeyed. "My friend," says he in his *Latter Day Pamphlets*, " do you think, had the united posterity of Adam voted, and since the Creation done nothing but vote, that three and three were seven, would this have altered the laws of arithmetic, or put to the blush the solitary Cocker who continued to assert privately that three and three were six? I consider not. And is arithmetic, think you, a thing more fixed by the Eternal than the laws of Justice are, and what the right is of man towards man? The builder of this World was Wisdom and Divine Foresight, not Folly and Chaotic Accident.

Eternal Law is silently present, everywhere and everywhen." And, again, he says, "Voting is a thing of little value at any time. If of ten men nine are recognisable as fools, how will you ever get a ballot-box to grind out a wisdom from their 'votes'?" Never by any conceivable ballot-box, nor by all the machinery in Bromwicham, or out of it, will you attain such a result."

A mind like this, so fierce and vehement, so lonely and out of tune with the age, yet with a "spirit of the largest size and divinest mettle" is truly one to make us pause and reflect. To see from his standpoint, and to judge rightly of the nature and value of his opinions, is not easy for us born with the traditions and prejudices of our age. "In looking at a man," he says somewhere, "out of the common, it is good for common men to make sure that they see before they attempt to oversee him." And again, "The eye sees only what it brings the means of seeing." And if to us he is cloudy and obscure, rhapsodical and mystical, let us consider the fault may be in us and not in him; and it would be well for those to reflect upon this who, though they have eyes, yet cannot see, but only scornfully elevate the eyebrow and use the curl of the lip form of rhetoric, before they pronounce the "poor stuff" they cannot understand in these *Latter Day Pamphlets* as the melancholy exhibition of a great genius. " Beware," says Goethe, " when the Great God lets loose a thinker on this planet then all things are at a risk."

In 1851 appeared *The Life of John Sterling*. This is one of the tenderest and most beautiful memorials ever raised to the memory of a man. It shows us Carlyle with his visor up, the large-hearted man and the warm, affectionate friend. Yet this biography ought never to have been written. It was given to the world in contradiction of another biography, prefaced to *Sterling's Remains*, by Archdeacon Hare, in which religious heterodoxy is made the great fact of Sterling's life. "A pale, sickly shadow in torn surplice" is presented, instead of the brilliant, beautiful, and cheerful John Sterling. "Why," asks Carlyle, "should this young, ardent spirit, 'a radiant child of the empyrean,' who perished manfully in the strife, why should he thus have been made a theological scarecrow? for this," he adds, "was the sin of Hare's book." Better that he should have gone to his rest in silence than to have had this misremembrance of him. It was to present another portrait that Carlyle undertook to write his life, and perhaps he has erred in the opposite direction in concealing from us the history of Sterling's struggles, how "he fought his doubts and gathered strength," and at last found that haven of rest for his soul which he so long desired to see. The last words Sterling ever wrote were indicative of a state of mind Carlyle has endeavoured to hide from us:—

> "Could we but hear all nature's voice
> From glow-worm up to sun,
> 'Twould speak with one concordant sound,
> Thy will, O God, be done!
> But hark! a sadder, mightier prayer,
> From all men's hearts that live—
> Thy will be done in earth and heaven,
> And Thou my sins forgive!"

This book is marred, also, by its mocking, depreciatory tone, and contemptuous scorn of things men deem sacred and holy, he classes them all under the category of shams, and calls them by such ugly names as "gibbering phantoms," "spectral inanities," "old clothes," or, again, as "huge unveracities and unrealities." One of the best things in this life is a sketch of Coleridge, and, excepting a touch of caricature, it is drawn with graphic vigour and force, though not flattering to Coleridge admirers. Another interesting study is that of Sterling's father, Captain Edward Sterling, "the Thunderer of *The Times* newspaper," whom Carlyle calls "Captain Whirlwind," an amazing, impetuous, hasty, explosive man, with a faculty of improvising, and capable of delivering three hundred and sixty-five opinions in the year on every subject. Sterling's letters (also those in Hare's life) are very interesting. The criticisms therein are exegetical, and give evidence of a richly endowed mind of remarkable vivacity and brilliancy, and they are perhaps as valuable as any part of his writings. Sterling said to Carlyle in one of his last letters—" Towards me it is still more true than towards England that no man has been and done like you." There is a deep significance in these words which would be well for such teachers as Carlyle to fully understand, for they are in this world spiritual lights, either for guidance or misguidance, and truly it may be said " our souls are in each others hands."

In 1865 was completed the *History of Frederick the Great*—Carlyle's last great work, which extended over 14 years of prodigious labour. This History has been more read and appreciated in Germany than here, and we doubt much whether the most enthusiastic admirers of Carlyle, in this country, will be able to see in the shabby, snuffy, shambling, lean-looking, old man, a king which they delight to honour—hard, narrow, tyrannical, and selfish as he was. Like many of Carlyle's heroes he can never be a lovable one. But Carlyle recognised him for the great work that he accomplished, as one of the chief creators of the Prussian Monarchy, who made the present greatness of Germany possible. What a man is must be estimated by what he does, and how much of his work will be productive in future ages. It is said that though Providence is always on the side of the strongest battalions, yet that the future belongs to the wisest. This is true, for the wisest and greatest in the world's history were not mere destroyers, but also creators. Herein is the difference between Frederick's work and Napoleon's. In this light we must read this remarkable history, judging the man by his merits, not by his defects; whether the real final result, when all the dross is purged away, is good. We must look at what Germany was before and after him, to fully appreciate the work that he did. Without such a pioneer it would have been impossible for our Teutonic neighbours to have risen to their present proud position among the nations.

In this world nothing "succeeds like success." And in Frederick's success is Carlyle's justification of his life and acts; for through life he has preached that no bad thing can succeed in the end. Even guided by this doctrine, we find it very hard to understand and justify such acts, for example, as the partition of Poland, which Carlyle describes as "the operations of Almighty Providence and the Eternal Laws of Nature." Thus he glosses over the doubtful means by which this success was obtained. But

Carlyle's passion for his hero is like that of a lover to his mistress. He cannot see any defects; and when he attempts a justification it is in awkward parenthesis, invoking the higher powers, and appealing to the Eternal Laws of the Universe. This History is too voluminous even for a very short notice. To us it is a weary task to follow these marches and counter-marches, battles and sieges, watching the moves, checks, and counter-checks in the mighty game of chess, with kings and emperors for the players. And it must have been desperate work for the historian to have fought all these battles over again, following his hero wearily and painfully sometimes, we think, day by day, week by week, and year by year with a painstaking and conscientiousness of detail through these interminable wars. Excepting in a few episodes, more especially in his early life, when he aspired to be a poet and a philosopher, it is only when, like the old "fighting Téméraire," he is towed into dock, his battles over, that we experience any sympathy towards him as a man. At other times he appears as a mere fighting machine. Yet he commenced life as a self-opinionated philanthrophist, though with rather sour and wilful notions of universal beneficence! Before he was king he had written a treatise, called the *Anti-Machiavel*, which was, says one of his biographers, "an edifying homily against rapacity, perfidy, arbitrary government, unjust war; in short, against almost everything for which its author is now remembered among men." The episodes in this history are most lively and amusing. The relations between Frederick and Voltaire are described by Carlyle with great gusto. He has revenged himself tenfold upon Voltaire for his scandalous life of Frederick and these memorable passages will live in History, even when "the dead past hath buried its dead."

We have thus far endeavoured to study the writings of this remarkable man. To the impartial mind there is much for serious consideration: but to merely read is to misunderstand them. As is the case of Richter, we want a lexicon to explain all the foreign words and peculiar modes of speech; for there is a significance, which is not seen at first, in those fantastic and unpronounceable words; and sometimes a sober meaning in those wild fancies, which in maniacal attitudes wander up and down the page, rioting in every form of expression. His writings are more critical, negative, and destructive than positive and reconstructive in their character; and they may be compared to some strong tower or grim fortress built more for strength and defence than for ornament and display.

In conclusion, we shall make a few general remarks upon the salient points of his teaching, more especially on his influence over our age as a religious teacher. It will, however, be necessary first for us to give his definition of what he calls religion, for of his creed we know nothing, though of his religious faith much. "It is well said, in every sense, that a man's religion is the chief fact, with regard to him, a man's or a nation of men's. By religion I do not mean the Church Creed which he professes, the Articles of Faith which he will sign and in words or otherwise assert, not this wholly, in many cases not this at all. We see men of all kinds of professed creeds attain to almost all degrees of worth or worthlessness under each or any of them. This is not what I call religion, this profession and assertion, which is often only a profession and assertion from the outworks of the man, from the mere argumentative region of him, if even so deep as that. But the thing a man does practically believe (and this is often enough without asserting it even to himself much less to others), the thing a man does practically lay to heart, and know for certain concerning his vital relations to this universe, and his duty and destiny there, that is in all cases the primary thing for him, and creatively determines all the rest. That is his religion."* According to Carlyle the master key to the whole moral nature is, What does a man secretly admire and worship? What fills him with the most earnest aspirations? What is the thing a man is infinitely afraid of, and struggles with his whole soul to escape from? The Heaven of succeeding, or the Hell of not succeeding in hte world (which belongs to the Gospel of Mammonism) is not the religion that Carlyle teaches. But it may be asked, What is his religion? What is his chief belief respecting the universe? If there is one truth Carlyle tries to enforce more than another it is the existence of a personal and over-ruling Deity, whom he calls upon men and nations to worship, and that so far and only so far as they have this faith are they wise in the true sense of wisdom. He does not attempt to prove the existence of a God, or reason about a probable God, but takes that for granted,

---

Lectures on Heroes and Hero-Worship.

holds it as self-evident and as the foundation and essence of all other truths; "endeavouring by logical argument to prove the existence of a God," he says with Kant, "would be like taking out a candle to look for the sun." Nay, gaze steadily into your candle-light, and the sun himself may be invisible. Religion is not of Sense but of Faith; not of Understanding but of Reason. He who finds himself without the latter, who by all his studying has failed to unfold it in himself, may have studied to great or to small purpose, we say not which; but of the Christian Religion, as of many other things, he has and can have no knowledge." He teaches us that there is a divine essence in man, and that religion must come from within and not from without; from the living spirit and not from the dead creed; that in our souls we shall find the clearest and only evidence that is worth anything of the truth and value of our faith, for our highest reverence and worship do not belong to knowledge but to faith and love. We could make many extracts from Carlyle's writings to prove that his faith corresponds with the faith of those who have given their testimony through life and death to that religion "which brought life and immortality to light," and which with all its difficulties (most of them based upon the necessary ignorance of man) explains a thousand difficulties philosophy alone could never have solved. In these days of inordinate speculation, of doubt and uncertainty, he tells us that religion is not a doubt, on the contrary it is a certainty or else a mockery and horror. On this point he expresses himself thus: "A man's religion consists not of the many things he is in doubt of, and tries to believe, but of the few he is assured of and has no need of effort for believing." Carlyle offers the best antidote to the philosophical speculations and scepticism of our age in the assertion "that conviction is worthless till it convert itself into conduct. Nay, properly, conviction is not possible till then; inasmuch as all speculation is by nature endless, formless, a vortex amid vortices: only by a felt, indubitable certainty of experience does it find any centre to revolve round, and so fashion itself into a system. Most true is it, as a wise man teaches us, that "Doubt of any sort cannot be removed except by Action." On which ground, too, let him who gropes painfully in darkness or uncertain light, and prays vehemently that the dawn may ripen into day, lay this other precept well to heart which to me was of invaluable service: "Do the duty which lies nearest thee which thou knowest to be a duty! Thy second duty will already have become clearer."* And here we touch another of Carlyle's great doctrines—that of the "sacredness of work."

In the Olympiad of life much is there to strive for and to conquer, and the soul is only made strong by conflict and wrestling. Live to act, and not to dream or to weave cobweb-speculations about happiness in this world or the next; study well each act, "for the gods themselves cannot annihilate the action done." "Cast forth," says Carlyle, "thy act, thy word, into the ever-living, ever-working universe: it is a seed-grain that cannot die; unnoticed to-day (says one), it will be found flourishing as a banyan grove (perhaps, alas! as a hemlock forest) after a thousand years."

---

* *Sartor Resartus.*

Thus to him our life is something more than a jest, and he addresses the time-killer, the mammon worshipper, the casino-loving mortal in some such language as that text in the Koran, "The heavens and the earth, and all that is between them, think ye they were created in jest?" Is this earth merely for you to sport and frolic your existence upon? No. "Your life is but a little gleam of time between two eternities; no second chance is given you for evermore. Sweep away all frothiness and falsehood from your heart, and struggle unweariedly to acquire what is possible for every man—a free, open, and humble soul." Perhaps the doctrine for which Carlyle has been most abused and misunderstood is the one so often associated with his name, that "Might is Right." He has been accused of being a blind idolater of brute force, a worshipper of success, &c. Carlyle does propound the doctrine that "Might is Right," but not in the vulgar meaning of the phrase. We will state his doctrine as concisely as we can. The Devil did not make this world, but God. He rules also, and only His work can succeed. Is not His name the All-mighty. Sentence of death is recorded against all error and falsehood in the world, and in that stern, deep battle between "Might and Right" we have but to await the issue. Yea, Might is Right,—the might of Truth, Wisdom, and Valour is ever the mightiest. All the strength of innumerable armies, with sword, steel, and cannon—the blaze of bonfires, with all the pomp, glory, and parade of the Universe—cannot support an unjust thing. "Await the issue. That which is right and just alone can have the victory. The cause thou fightest for, so far as it is true, no further, yet precisely so far, is sure of victory. The falsehood alone of it will be conquered, will be abolished, as it ought to be; but the truth of it is part of Nature's own laws, co-operates with the world's eternal tendencies, and cannot be conquered."

WIT AND HUMOUR.

"Man could direct his ways by plain reason, and support his life by tasteless food; but God has given us wit, and flavour, and brightness, and laughter, and perfumes, to enliven the days of man's pilgrimage and to 'charm his pained steps over the burning marl.'"—*Rev. Sydney Smith.*

"What a dull, plodding, tramping, clanking would the ordinary intercourse of Society be without wit to enliven and brighten it!"—*Archdeacon Hare.*

" As long liveth the merry man, they say,
 As doth the sorry man, and longer by a day."
 . . . . . .
" Another sayd sawe doth men advise,
 That they be together both merry and wise."
     Old Comedy, " *Ralph Roister Doister,*"
         Published 1566.

WIT AND HUMOUR.

MAN is the only animal to whom has been given the faculty of laughing. This is one of the many valuable privileges Nature has bestowed upon him. Laughter is a most healthful exercise; and the man who has not the faculty to perceive the ludicrous, nor a healthy secretion of good humour in his nature, suffers both in body and mind—becomes dyspeptic and melancholic; for laughter assists digestion, and clears off bad humours from the brain. " Laughter," says Dr. Hufeland, "is one of the greatest helps to digestion with which I am acquainted; and the custom prevalent among our forefathers of exciting it at table by jesters and buffoons, was founded on true medical principles." Harvey, the discoverer of the circulation of the blood, says: "When the regions about the thorax and lungs are stimulated by laughter, the system resumes, &c., and the arterial vessels perform their functions with ease." But we need not multiply medical testimony to a fact that is obvious. We can almost fancy some doctor of the future prescribing to his patient a dose of laughter, and when taken to be well shaken, so as fully to realize the poet's description of "Laughter holding both his sides."

Laughter is the music of a glad heart; and "a merry heart," says Solomon, "is the life of the flesh; for gladness prolongeth the days of a man." Milton, the stern Puritan poet, speaks of that "vein of laughing which hath oft-times a strong and sinewy face in teaching and comforting."

He who has never laughed, hath never loved; for love is the well-spring of mirth and good humour. "No man," says an eminent author, "who has heartily and wholly laughed, can be altogether and irreclaimably bad. How much lies in laughter — the cypher-key wherewith we decipher the whole nature.' "Shun," says Lavater, "the man who never laughs, who dislikes music and the glad face of a child." Most of us have felt a chill as of the coldest winter in the presence of the man who cannot laugh, who presents to you a perfect dead wall of countenance, whose eye meets yours with a stony stare, and whose smile is like the "cold glitter of ice." Let us pity him, for he is utterly incapable of any noble thought or feeling—for his heart is as "dry as summer's dust." We imagine it must have been of such an one that Shakespeare wrote—" He was like a man made after supper of a cheeseparing."

Equally unpleasant is the presence of the man who, in the severe asperity of his nature, would drown laughter in tears, who would cloud the sunny face of childhood with sorrow, would hang this beautiful world round with pictures of misery and despair, put beauty and hope in a coffin, and look at the world through funeral crape.

There are others who, in their plethoric vanity, regard a hearty laugh as vulgar in the extreme; as, for instance, that dainty specimen of the *genus homo*—the conceited, simpering, tiptoeing, oiled and perfumed dandy of the modern Dundreary type, whose face, like his linen, is never out of starch, and who is as incapable of laughing as he is of thinking. "Such an one, when drest out," says Sir Thomas Overbury, "reminds us of the cinnamon tree—the bark is of more value than the body."

Our last specimen is the man who never condescends to laugh — who, with a supercilious pedantry, struts about on the stilts of his own importance,—who would make us believe that he carries the world, like Atlas, upon his shoulders, and all goodness under his beaver. "I am Sir Oracle," says he; "and when I ope my mouth, let no dog bark." Like the poor quack, who has just wit enough to see through those, who cannot see through him, whose serious face is part of his stock-in-trade, he passes off this gravity for wisdom—a very bad pretension, as the ass is said to have the gravest face in creation. So much for his show of wisdom!

Laughter is good, and wise men have loved it. It is one of God's best gifts to man. For our own part, we love to hear, not only the loud ringing laughter of childhood, as it lifts its head and tosses back its curls, with a face like a young radiant Apollo; but also the hoarse, broken laughter of the old man, though at times, liked a cracked bell, it has a mournful sound.

> " The young they laugh ; laughs not the sky?
> The winds they laugh, as they pass by.
> The sun, he laughs; and Nature's face
> Beams with a joyous, laughing grace."

Give us, then, the free, open, and hearty laugh; not a laugh merely outside the teeth, or to "sniff and titter, and snigger from the throat outwards"—a laugh, not of the face and diaphragm only, "but of the whole man, from head to heel," till altogether he shakes like a jelly. As we cannot always laugh, though nature has given us more provocatives for the exercise of this faculty than any other, let us "laugh when we can and cry when we must."

In making these observations upon laughter, we wish not to be misunderstood. Our subject is partial; it will take up only *one side*, and that not the serious side, of human life. We must remember that life is not a jest, that to laugh is not to live; and that frequent laughing has been long called a sign of a little mind; or, in other words, it is the foolish who laughs foolishly. The man who laughs at everything, we should deem frivolous or simple. But he who habitually laughs at the misfortunes of others (if we ought to call that a laugh which springs from heartless malignity) is irreclaimably bad.

Again, let a man do the duty nearest to him, which God has ordained him to do in this world, manfully and hopefully, without the fear of the laughter of others, for ridicule, like salt, falls harmlessly upon us, unless we have sore places. Let him endeavour to lead a good and noble life; keep a mind open and pure, and free from envy. Let him cherish faith, hope, love, and that divine resignation which will help to wean him gently from life and fit him to die smiling.

There is a beautiful sentiment, translated from the Persian, by Sir William Jones, which perhaps, will not be out of place to quote here. It runs thus—

> "On parent knees a naked, new-born child
> Weeping thou sat'st, while all around thee smiled,
> So live, that sinking in thy last, long sleep
> Calm thou may'st smile, while all around thee weep."

It will be impossible for us to study the broad subject of mirth in its infinite varieties. We shall consider its various aspects, more especially as they are related to the subject of Wit and Humour.

In our lives the sublime and the ridiculous are closely blended. Laughter and tears, joy and sorrow, are the opposite sides of human life; yet so closely are they allied that, like pleasure and pain, one seems to spring from the other, for the "source of laughter is close to the fountain of tears."

These two principles, though contrary, run in and out, cross and re-cross each other, and form the mingled yarn of that coloured web we call life.

> "Joy and woe are woven fine,
> A clothing for the soul divine.
> Under every grief and pine
> Runs a joy with silken twine."
>
> W. BLAKE.

Though laughing and crying are contrary effects, the least alteration of features occasions the difference. Reubens, it is said, by a single stroke, could change a laughing face into a crying one. For it is but turning up the muscles to laugh, and down to cry. And it is said of a celebrated actor of the last century, that he could in a moment, as by the stroke of a magician's wand, change the laughter of his audience into tears.

Shakespeare—to whom every avenue of the human heart

was known—prepares us for the darkest scenes in his tragedies (like a kind friend communicating to us sad tidings) by gently humouring our fancies before the last dread scene. He places his fools, who are the scape-goats of his wit and the safety-valves of his humour, side by side with kings, queens, princes, nobles, and cardinals, and, in the darkest crimes, the fools' humours and jests light the way "even to dusky death." The facetious grave-digger in "Hamlet" propounds his riddles —moralizes in a humorous strain, takes a battered skull for his text, and sings of the days when even he could love (fancy a grave-digger in love!); this he does over the grave of the broken-hearted Ophelia.

It is from no spirit of revelry or caprice this strange juxtaposition takes place. The man of humour, by an intuitive perception, discovers beneath the surface of things those ever-working heterogeneous elements which produce those strange contrasts and grotesque accompaniments through all the moving, acting, suffering, and laughing forms of our real life—the sports, freaks, gambols of mother Nature with her children, with also "the drivelling, squinting, sprawling, clowneries of nature," and all her abominations, "worse than fables, yet have feigned, or fear conceived."

It is only the wit and humorist who can present to us truly the follies, fancies, and manners of this world we live in. They have their legitimate sphere of action in detecting the counterfeit forms of life, in exposing falsehood and error; and their influence is necessary for the equilibrium of forces in the moral world, when the moral atmosphere is dark and lowering, when vice and folly are triumphant, and the stormy wind of men's passions, like "blasts from hell," burn and devastate the earth, when superstition lifts up her dark banner, stained with the innocent blood of martyrs, and the weary eyes of men look upward to HIM who alone in HIS Omnipotence seems secure—it is then the satirist, from the fierce tempest of his indignant soul, sends forth his shafts of wit "dipt in scorn's fiery poison," which, like lightning, "can transfix bigotry and tyranny, can strike its object over thousands of miles of space, across thousands of years of time, and which, through its sway over the universal weakness of man, is an everlasting instrument to make the bad tremble and the foolish to wince."

> "Nor martyr-flames, nor trenchant swords,
> Can do away that ancient lie;
> A gentler death shall Falsehood die,
> Shot thro' and thro' with cunning words."

Wit is the greatest counterfeit detector in the world. Falsehood cannot abide its truth, for it corrodes and eats off that fine plated surface, and shows the fraud. It can detect and expose sophisms which elude the most subtle and serious reasoning. How often is the seemingly strongest logical position destroyed by a single stroke of wit, and, when reason fails, we find our last recourse in ridicule, which sometimes fails also, as there are some natures upon whom reason and wit are spent in vain, they being simply impenetrable. "Against stupidity," says Schiller, "the gods strive in vain." How often do we find that the man who is the loudest, most persistent, and bigoted, in what he calls *his* opinions, the more childish his reasons are, the more hopeless he is to convince on that account. Such men never reason truly, because they never think, but maintain a singular existence, without the slightest exercise of their reasoning faculties. We have read of an amusing instance of solid impenetrability which, perhaps, is peculiar to the British mind. "It is said that Dr. Johnson, once at a Lord Mayor's dinner, committed the scandalous impropriety of talking wit and wisdom to an alderman by his side, who desired to concentrate his whole energies on the turtle. 'Sir,' said the alderman, in a tone and with a look of awful rebuke, 'in attempting to listen to your long sentences, and give you a short answer, I have swallowed two pieces of green fat without tasting the flavour. I beg you to let me enjoy my present happiness in peace.'"

Sometimes wit strikes like the lightning-flash, to shiver and blast, like the fiery-hot scorching satires of Juvenal; or like the sunbeam, to penetrate the hidden recesses of folly and superstition. Sometimes, as in Pope, it is a rod for the fool's back; at another, as in Swift, like the cool, keen knife of the murderer. Sometimes it penetrates its victim with its glittering shafts, like the Indian method of torture by impaling with needles. Or it applies the scourge to those false professors of religion, who, according to Swift, "have just enough religion to make them hate, and not enough to make them love each other." Burns' "Holy Willie's Prayer" is an example of this. Sometimes wit administers wisdom, and gives the best advice where least expected—as, when some one asked Tom Cribb which was the best attitude for self-defence, "To keep a civil tongue in your head," was the reply. Sometimes wit administers wisdom in high places, and even the fool is wiser than the monarch—as, when Henry the Eighth, after writing his book upon the "Seven Sacraments" (a book of wonderful erudition and orthodoxy), and the title of "Defender of the Faith" having been conferred upon him by the Pope; flushed with exultation, he met his fool, and turning to him, said, "Fool, they have made me 'Defender of the Faith.'" "Oh! good Harry," said the fool, "let us each defend one another, for I am sure the true faith is able to defend itself." Thus we see that even the poor fool in his day had his uses, for *his* was often the only privileged tongue about the Court. Dr. Fuller, speaking of Queen Elizabeth's fool, says that " he told the Queen more of her faults than most of her chaplains, and cured her melancholy better than all her physicians."

Sometimes wit startles us with contrasts, by comparing facts—as when Voltaire remarks that Penn's treaty with the Indians was the only one ever made between civilized men and savages not sanctioned by an oath, and the only one that ever was kept. Sometimes wit makes sport of argument, and by sharp repartee slaps conviction in the face—as when some cynic, in disparaging marriage, called it, even at best, a mere cat and dog life. "But," said a young hopeful, "cats and dogs sometimes live quietly and happily together." "Yes," said the wit, not at all abashed, in reply, "but tie them together." Sometimes wit rejoices in an *apt* simile, and hits off an unpleasant truth in an apposite and pleasant way—as when Swift says, "that the reason why so few marriages are happy, is because young ladies spend so much time in making nets, not in making cages." Wit, again, will take down the insolence and conceit of the nobodies who think themselves somebodies. "He is a a *self-made* man," said one in praise of an all-sufficient insufficient person. "Yes," was the reply, "and he adores his *Maker*."

Humour we might compare to the warm sunshine, which melts the cold, glittering frost of conventionality and bathes everything, both high and low, in its beams. It is the richest unction of the mind—now oozing through the roguish twinkling of the eye, or bursting through the floodgates of laughter; it pours sweetness, not gall, into the cup of humanity. Wit and Humour, although closely allied, are distinct in their functions. "Humour," says Thackeray, "is the union of wit with love." Wit exists by *antipathy*, humour by *sympathy*. Wit is often the product of contempt; humour springs from love. Wit laughs *at* things; humour laughs *with* them. "It chastens the dangerous faculty of wit, turning its envenomed shafts into instruments of healing." Wit can sneer, growl, hate, and destroy; but, unlike humour, it cannot cheer, it cannot create or communicate the life of love. Carlyle says, "that humour is properly the exponent of low things; that which first renders them poetical to the mind. The man of humour sees common life, even mean life, under the new light of sportfulness and love; whatever has existence has a charm for him. Humour has justly been regarded as the finest perfection of poetic genius. He who wants it, be his other gifts what they may, has only half a mind, an eye for what is above him, not for what is about him or below him."

Humour is the twin-sister of pathos; hand in hand they go together. Nature never created a laughing philosopher without a crying one, and sometimes she unites them both. "There are merry books which set you weeping when the sun shines," and "melancholy books which make you laugh." Truly there is a mirth in melancholy, and the worst melancholy is that which comes after a surfeit of laughter. Humour is sometimes as with Cowper, "a sad heart's sunshine." "If I trifle," said he, in one of his letters, "and merely trifle, it is because I am reduced to it by necessity; a melancholy that nothing else so effectually disperses engages me sometimes in the arduous task of being merry by force; and, strange as it may seem, the most ludicrous lines I ever wrote have been written in the saddest mood, and but for that saddest mood, perhaps, had never been written at all." "Humour is a word," says Mr. Taine, "untranslateable in French, because in France they have not the idea. Humour is a species of talent which amuses Germans, Northmen, it suits their mind as beer suits their palate; for men of another race it is disagreeable—they often find it too harsh and bitter." It seems strange that two nations, separated only by a "silver streak of sea," should so little understand each other. The Frenchman delights in picturing the English as sour and melancholy, solitary and sad, which he attributes to our climate. He has described us as "having one hundred religions and only one sauce:" certainly he is nearly the opposite to us in that respect. Years ago Froissart said of the English, "they take their pleasure sadly;" and Voltaire says somewhere "that in London there are days when the wind is in the east when it is customary for people to hang themselves by the neck in parks and places of amusement." We who can understand the Frenchman better than he can understand us, are not surprised that if he cannot find the word Home in his vocabulary he should seek in vain for the word Humour also, for the chief attributes of mirth and humour are composed of those affections which cluster around our hearts and homes.

A sense of incongruity lies often at the root of the ludicrous. Bulls, blunders, and anachronisms, though they often belong to the region of stupidity, always produce laughter: take the following specimen of an Irish bull, quoted by Sydney Smith: "An English gentleman was writing a letter in a coffee-house, and perceiving that an Irishman stationed behind him was taking that liberty which Parmenio used with his friend Alexander, instead of putting his seal upon the lips of the curious impertinent, the English gentleman thought proper to reprove the Hibernian, if not with delicacy at least with poetical justice. He concluded writing his letter in these words: 'I would say more, but a d——d tall Irishman is reading over my shoulder every word I write.' 'You lie, you scoundrel!' said the self-convicted Hibernian." .

In painting alone there is a rich harvest of anachronisms. Burgoyne, in his travels, notices a painting in Spain where Abraham is preparing to shoot Isaac with a blunderbuss. A painter who evidently did not pride himself in his severe realism, in representing the miracle of St. Anthony preaching to the fishes, painted the lobsters, in the attitude of listening, *red*. Being asked why he did not paint them their natural colour, he justified himself by saying that the whole affair was a *miracle*, and that the miracle was made still greater. A large volume might be written upon the errors and anachronisms of our best authors, including, Homer, Shakespeare, Milton, &c., and especially in the writings of our greatest critics.

Dr. Barrow, in one of his sermons, has perhaps better

than any other writer attempted to trace the springs of laughter to their source in his celebrated description of facetiousness. "Sometimes," he says, "it lieth in pat allusion to a known story, or in seasonable application of a trivial saying, or in forging an apposite tale; sometimes it playeth in words and phrases, taking advantage from the ambiguity of their sense or the affinity of their sound. Sometimes it is wrapped in a dress of luminous expression; sometimes it lurketh under an odd similitude. Sometimes it is lodged in a sly question, in a smart answer, in a quirkish reason, in a shrewd intimation, in cunningly diverting or cleverly retorting an objection. Sometimes it is couched in a bold scheme of speech, in a tart irony, in a startling metaphor, in a plausible reconciling of contradictions, or in acute nonsense. Sometimes a scenical representation of persons or things, a counterfeit speech —a mimical look or gesture passeth for it. Sometimes an affected simplicity. Sometimes a presumptuous bluntness gives it being. Sometimes it riseth only from a lucky hitting upon what is strange. Sometimes from a crafty wresting obvious matter to the purpose. Often it consisteth in one knows not what, and springeth up one can hardly tell how. Its ways are unaccountable and inexplicable, being answerable to the numberless rovings of fancy and windings of language." Following this unique description, we may say also that it twists, jerks, and tosses words into every conceivable shape of sense and nonsense, now bursting out into a fiery shower of puns, or making one rhyme trip upon the heels of another, in all

"The extravagancy
And crazy ribaldry of fancy."

The literature of mirth is wide and varied—from the

laughter of the ancients, which has echoed through centuries, down to the last syllable of a joke recorded in *Punch*. We shall only be able to notice a few of the great wits and humorists—such is the wide range and extent of our subject. For to mirth is to be attributed the easy, smiling, courtly satires of Horace; the light, airy, grotesque buffooneries of Aristophanes; the matchless irony of Lucian; the fun which reels about, among the darker passions, in the drunken revelries of Rabelias; the wide-world laughter of Shakespeare; the scoffing satires of Butler; the genial fun of Addison; the polished and glittering shafts of Pope; the fierce invective of Swift; the sky-raking, star-spangling merriment of Moore; the fun, frolic, and playfulness of Charles Lamb; the elephantine laughter of Carlyle; the warm, comfortable, yet sly, insinuating humour of Dickens; and last, but not least, the jokes of that red-faced old reveller, the Momus of English Literature, *Punch*, whose eye twinkles with roguish mirth and fun, who laughs at everybody and everything, and belabours with his club every abuse within his reach.

One of the *wisest* of men, viz., Shakespeare, was also one of the *merriest*. In studying his biography through his writings—and it is there we get the best glimpses into his inner life, which is confirmed by what we know of his outer life—one can there discern a man of infinite wit and humour, who loved a merry jest among his friends, "who was rich in quick bouts of merry argument," and "witty sallies quenched in laughter sweet." Fair, ripe jokes, mellowed by the sunshine of his humour, hang about his pages in rich profusion. He has truly represented to us all the witchery of the poet's fancy:—

> "Quips and cranks and wanton wiles,
> Nods and becks and wreathed smiles ;
> Sport that wrinkled care derides,
> And laughter holding both his sides."

Look at Falstaff, that huge mass of gluttony and cowardice, stuffed full of pomposity and pretence; yet withal a very monument of mirth, a monster of fat and humour, shaking the earth's sides with its elephantine roar. Among the wits of the last century two, viz., Swift and Pope, stand pre-eminent. Swift's writings are a cold-blooded satire upon human nature, and even upon himself—a dark, scornful, and impure spirit; his laugh was like the laugh of a fiend that saw everything in the gleam and glare of infernal light. "He was made," as Fuller said of Pasquil, "all of tongue and teeth, biting whatever he touched, and it bled whatever he bit." Truly melancholy is the picture of that man's life and death. Shut up in his own solitary, miserable self he looked at the world with fiery, blood-shot eyes, and through his writings poured out the venom of his merciless, vindictive malice and scorn upon mankind, and at last, as he anticipated, "died in a rage, like a poisoned rat in a hole."

Pope was of a different spirit. Of a shy, sensitive, yet combative nature, nervous temperament and delicate constitution, with keen morbid sensibilities, he smarted and writhed under the spiteful attacks of the meanest scribbler in Grub Street, and too often wasted the great powers of his mind in conferring immortality upon dunces. In his satires, and more especially in his *Dunciad*, he has shown all the nervous hatred and hearty contempt he felt for cant, feebleness of thought, stupidity, and commonplace—in short, for all shapes and shades of dulness. Against these he has used all the deadly arms of verbal warfare, and subjected their unhappy authors to every variety of critical torture—he riddles them with epigrams, he scorches them with his sarcasm, and views their ludicrous agonies with mocking glee. It is an old saying "that a blow from a word strikes deeper than a blow with a sword." Pope knew his power, and triumphantly could exclaim :—

> "I own I'm proud, I must be proud, to see
> Men not afraid of GOD afraid of me."

In studying the literature of the present century we cannot fail to observe that it has taken a decidedly comic turn, which is fast sweeping away that whining sentimental "*Satanic School*," as Southey called it, in which the predominant principle is a morbid voluptuousness, composed of sensuality and noble sentiments, unreal mockeries of men and women. The acknowledged idol of this school is some poor moon-struck, sentimental fool, who mistakes his melancholy madness for inspiration, and who raves, howls, and screams at what the Americans call "the calm facts of the universe." Much of this change is to be attributed to Hood and Dickens. The latter has touched the secret chords of our nature, and sounded a hearty, healthful response. His characters are painted, not in fashionable rouge, but in the healthy bloom of activity and life. We have laughed, and laugh still, at the infinite resources of his humour, his most excellent fancy, and wept over his touches of deep pathos. His writings are what Emerson calls "blood-warm," and one feels him to be a brother man. From the time of his writing "Pickwick," when he inundated London with laughter, down to his latest writings, he has written much for us to laugh, less for us to weep, and nothing for us to blush at. He has studied low life, and depicted to us the humours of the streets, and no one knew the street life of London better; here he was at home. We thank him for one hearty and generous sentiment, which we quote, because it refers particularly to our subject. "It is," he says, "a fair, even-handed, noble adjustment of things, that while there is infection in disease and sorrow, there is nothing so irresistibly contagious as mirth and good-humour."

Hood was essentially a humorist, one who could play with the lighter foibles of human nature, and make us laugh at them until we loved them the more, as being inseparable from our common humanity. He could make us laugh until our laughter dissolved in burning tears a-down our cheeks—could make even a jest reveal to us a startling, fearful fact. He makes us laugh at what is odd, strange, and grotesque, but at what is vile—never. In his humour is mixed the grave and gay, the mirthful and sad. "He casts his melancholy into shapes so fantastic" (says Gilfillan) "that they lure first himself and then his hearers into laughter. If he cannot get rid of that grim, gigantic shadow of himself, which walks ever before him, he can, at least, make mouths and cut antics behind its back." If fortune goes hard against him, like Richter, he can keep laughing at her face till she ceased frowning at him. Look at his life, a life as he once humorously said "Notorious for enjoying bad health," afflicted for twenty years with a complication of disorders, confined to his chamber as rigidly as if it had been a cell in Pentonville Penitentiary; working in a wretched garret, "with the naked tiles above and the barren boards below," writing, as he says, for the magazines long-winded articles, with weakly lungs, with hunger like a ravening wolf at his door, spinning out his body like a spider, until at last "he did look like a spider, with long spindle legs, and only a dot of a body in the middle." But for all this keeping up a hopeful, cheerful, and even mirthful spirit, knowing as he did that that forlorn attic was but the type of a more dreadful destitution — an unfurnished mind. Look at him broken down in body, but not in spirit, and it seems a subject of wonderment from whence those rich streams of humour could flow. Speaking from his chamber, hear how lightly he could talk of the ills which surround an invalid powerless in the hands of captious nurses:—"A more serious peril from illness concerns the temper. When the nerves are irritable and the stomach is irritable, not to be irritable altogether is a moral miracle. For example, after soot in your gruel, tallow-grease in your barley-water, and snuff over your light pudding, to have 'the draught as before' poured into your wakeful eyes, instead of your open mouth, by a drunken Mrs. Gamp, or one of her stamp; to check at such a moment the explosive speech is, at least, equal to spiking a cannon in the heat of battle. There is beyond denial an ease to the chest or somewhere in a passionate objurgation; so much so that a certain invalid of our acquaintance, doubly afflicted with a painful complaint and an unmanageable, hard-mouthed temper, regularly retains, as helper to the sick-nurse, a stone deaf old woman whom he can abuse without violence to her feelings." In another place he says, "Are we, therefore, miserable, hypped, disconsolate? Answer, ye book-shelves, whence we draw the consolations of Philosophy, the dreams of poetry and romance, the retrospections of history, and glimpses of society from the better novels. Mirth, comfort, and entertainment even for these small hours become so long from an unhealthy vigilance. Answer, ye pictures and prints, a portrait gallery of Nature!—and reply in your own tones, dear old Fiddle, so often tuned to one favourite sadly-sweet air, and the words of Curran:—

> "But since in wailing
> There's nought availing,
> But death unfailing
> Must strike the blow,—
> Then for this reason,
> And for a season,
> Let us be merry before we go."

Truly this was an heroic life, indicating a mind serene, cheerful, hopeful, and unconquered by physical pain. Hood has been sneered at as a Cockney poet, as if there were nothing in the mighty heart of London to inspire a great poet. London itself is a grand epic poem, where are to be found materials for the deepest tragedy, as well as for the finest and broadest comedy.

Great is the poet who can interpret to us nature's mysteries and unravel her seeming intricacies, speaking out to the listening world in grand eloquent music the weird meaning of her mystic characters. The calm floating clouds, with their ever-shifting scenes moving in the sea of blue overhead; the golden tears of heaven, which men call stars; the storm, the calm, the sunshine, the pleasant eve, the cloud-capped mountains, and fruitful valleys, the dim moonlight drapery, and glories of the setting sun, the chant-music of the winds, and the ever-throbbing ocean beating the pulse of the earth—all these he mingles in his sacred lore, and sets to music to gladden the hearts of his fellow men. But greater still, we think, is the poet who can enter into the dark, struggling sea of human life, where the groans of the captive, the wailings of the oppressed, the sufferings of the great and good, the cry of the widowed mother and the orphan are heard. Has the Poet no mission there, as Sandy Mackaye says, "Is there no heaven above them there, and the hell beneath them? And God frowning and the devil grinning? No poetry there! Is no the verra idea of the classic tragedy defined to be, man conquered by circumstance? Canna ye see it there? And the verra idea of the modern tragedy, man conquering circumstance? And I'll show you that too—in mony a garret where no eye but the gude God's enters, to see the patience, and the fortitude, and the self-sacrifice, and the love stronger than death, that's shining in the dark places o' the earth." Truly, the Cockney poet hath a mission if he cannot "babble o' green fields," wild flowers, and sunny water brooks, he can depict the humours of the streets, where we meet with odd groups, queer faces, grotesque forms, and laughable incidents at every step over which Humour born of Pathos can pour its floods of genial mirth.

Charles Lamb, another of the once stigmatised Cockney Poets, was a humorist of the first order, and an example, like Hood, of a brave heart manfully fronting a sea of troubles without being overwhelmed, and with this difference, that in Lamb's case, a mind diseased* had to minister to itself and to find its own consolation and remedy. There is something very touching in the record of these two quiet heroic lives (Lamb and his sister's), the full measure of their suffering, patience, and endurance is known to God alone; but Lamb learned early cheerfully to submit to his destiny, and to make it his duty. He was a wayward genius, a sport of nature, one that we cannot classify and label, his eccentricities were original and personal, and connected with his "sympathies, apathies, and antipathies," which came out in all kinds of whims and oddities, such as saying a grace before Milton and Shakespeare, saluting old Chapman's "Homer" with a kiss, or hissing with the rest his own farce when it was damned on the first night of its performance. His writings are impressions of himself, of his frolicsome and almost crazy humour, his horror of cant hypocrisy, and the stupidly good. Among his friends he would stammer out his puns like minute guns, or open upon them a small battery of cynical epigrams; or if he had a philosopher at table would carry on an argument with laughter, against all the rules of common sense, slyly interposing paradoxes which would convert logic into nonsense and nonsense into logic. Like nearly all our great humorists who seem to breathe more freely the air of cities, life, bustle, and society were as necessary to him as his daily bread. And when in his last days it became necessary, for the sake of his sister's

---

* There was a tendency to insanity in his family, and at one period of his life he had been confined in an asylum.

health as well as his own, to remove into the country he pined, moped, and longed for his old town life, with its hot suppers and late hours. Writing to Wordsworth he said, "What have I gained by health? Intolerable dulness: What by early hours and moderate meals? A total blank." He delighted to tease Wordsworth by professing to hold in contempt what was most dear to him—his love of solitude and nature. "Separate from the pleasure of your company," he says, "I don't much care if I never see a mountain in my life. I have passed all my days in London, until I have formed as many and intense local attachments as any of you mountaineers can have done with dead nature. The lighted shops of the Strand and Fleet Street; the innumerable trades, tradesmen, and customers, coaches, waggons, playhouses, all the bustle and wickedness round about Covent Garden; the watchmen, drunken scenes, rattles—life awake if you awake at all hours of the night; the impossibility of being dull in Fleet Street; the crowds, the very dirt and mud, the sun shining upon houses and pavements, the print shops, the old bookstalls, parsons cheapening books, coffee-houses, steams of soups from kitchens, the pantomimes—London itself a pantomime and a masquerade—all these things work themselves into my mind and feed me without a power of satiating me. The wonder of these sights impels me into night-walks about her crowded streets, and I often shed tears in the motley Strand from fulness of joy at so much life. All these emotions must be strange to you; so are your rural emotions to me. But, consider, what must I have been doing all my life not to have lent great portions of my heart with usury to such scenes?" Yet Wordsworth could say of Lamb, "Oh, he was good, if e'er a good man lived."

As a specimen of Lamb's happiest humour, we give an extract from one of his letters to Bernard Barton; the poet, we suppose, had complained to him of his liver, and Lamb gives him this consolation: "You are too much apprehensive of your complaint; I know many that are always ailing of it, and live on to a good old age. I know a merry fellow (you partly know him), who, when his medical adviser told him he had drunk away all *that part*, congratulated himself (now his liver has gone) that he should be the longest liver of the two.

"The best way in these cases is to keep yourself as ignorant as you can, as ignorant as the world was before Galen, of the inner construction of the animal man; not to be conscious of a midriff; to hold kidneys (save those of sheep and swine) to be an agreeable fiction; not to know whereabouts the gall grows; to account the circulation of the blood an idle whimsey of Harvey's; to acknowledge no mechanism not visible. For once fix the seat of your disorder, and your fancies flux into it like bad humours. Those medical gentries choose each his favourite part; one takes the lungs, another the aforesaid liver, and refer to that, whatever in the animal economy is amiss. Above all, use exercise, take a little more spirituous liquors, learn to smoke, continue to keep a good conscience, and avoid tampering with hard terms of art—viscosity, scirrhosity, and those bugbears by which simple patients are scared into their graves. Believe the general sense of the mercantile world, which holds that desks are not deadly. It is the mind, good B. B., and not the limbs, that taints by long sitting. Think of the patience of tailors, think how long the Lord Chancellor sits, think of the brooding hen."

As one of the wittiest of our wits, and most humorous of our humorists, we ought not to pass over Sydney Smith—"a joker of jokes,' yet withal one who possessed a strong, healthy, shrewd, vigorous mind, a clear, logical brain, and a warm honest English heart, which could detect and hate deformity, cruelty, bigotry, and fraud in any shape. As a "witty pamphleteer," and a contributor to the *Edinburgh Review*, he wrote a number of articles upon the political and social questions of the day, which are remarkable for their sterling wit and genuine humour, sound logic, and, what is more rare, common sense (for nothing is more *uncommon* than common sense). Every subject he has treated in his own way, and from his own peculiar point of view, and with such verbal felicity, that we can even now read them without fear of dulness. His wit may be best described as sharp, stinging common sense, which he throws like darts at his opponents. His logic swims and glistens in mirth, and in his humour he is like a leviathan in sport, rolling and tossing everything in a sea of laughter. We will make one selection from his writings from an article upon "Waterton's Wanderings in South America," where he endeavours to reconcile us to our much-abused English climate, by showing the disadvantages of tropical climates arising from animals and insects. "Every animal," he says, "has his enemies. The land tortoise has two enemies—man and the boa constrictor. Man takes him home and roasts him, and the boa constrictor swallows him whole, shell and all, and consumes him slowly in the interior, as the Court of

Wit and Humour.

Chancery does a great estate. Insects," he adds a few sentences after, "are the curse of tropical climates. The bête rouge lays the foundation of a tremendous ulcer. In a moment you are covered with ticks. Chigoes bury themselves in your flesh, and hatch a large colony of young chigoes in a few hours. They will not live together, but every chigoe sets up a separate ulcer, and has his own private portion of pus. Flies get into your mouth, into your eyes, into your nose; you eat flies, drink flies, and breathe flies. Lizards, cockroaches, and snakes get into the bed; ants eat up the books; scorpions sting you on the foot. Everything bites, stings, or bruises; every second of your existence you are wounded by some piece of animal life that nobody has ever seen before, except Swammerdam and Merian. An insect with eleven legs is swimming in your tea cup, a nondescript with nine wings is struggling in the small beer, or a caterpillar with several dozen eyes in his belly is hastening over the bread and butter. All nature is alive, and seems to be gathering all her entomological hosts to eat you up, as you are standing, out of your coat, waistcoat, and breeches. Such are the tropics. All this reconciles us to our dews, fogs, vapours, and drizzle—to our apothecaries rushing about with gargles and tinctures—to our old British constitutional coughs, sore throats, and swelled faces."

We feel that in this short space we have not done justice to our subject; there are other names, some perhaps more worthy, which might have been mentioned; we have not forgotten Burns, Byron, Moore, Thackeray, Jerrold, De Quincey, and many others who have enriched our literature with their humorous creations and characters. We might have introduced you to the witty and comprehensive Christopher North—to those meetings at Ambroses. Rare and pleasant must those meetings have been which sometimes took place, although not in regular nights! What subjects, human or divine, could have escaped their notice when Christopher North, the master of the revels, presided? —what flashes of wit emanated from their brains by jerking contact—what floods of mirth must have gushed forth in rich streams of humour, and ever and anon there arose glorious islets, sunned by the gleam—

> "The light that never was on sea or land,
> The consecration and the poet's dream."

But now, alas! the charmed circle is broken. The bright comic face of Wilson, once a very disc of mirth, is now eclipsed, and the hollow orb of that bright eye, which once contained a world of laughter, is now sightless and dim. The Ettrick Shepherd is gone to his rest; Lockhart, De Quincey, and the others have followed him. Time leaves its dark shadow on the wall, as death takes away the gifted and the noble:

> "Come away; no more of mirth
> Is here, or merry-making sound.
> The house was builded of the earth,
> And shall fall again to ground."

In conclusion, let us say that these men—the wits and humorists—have had, and still have, their work to do in this world. As long as corruption and knavery exist—as long as passion tempts, sloth enfeebles, fear degrades, power threatens, and oppression reigns—these men will have their uses—to arouse and guide our love and sympathy

—our pity for the weak, the poor, and the suffering—our scorn for insolence and pretension, for what is false, mean, and base. And though their weapons are sometimes misused and misdirected, and from their hearts sometimes proceed scoffing or ribaldry, where there ought to be reverence and love, yet let us be thankful for what their genius has left us as a priceless bequest—for their glee, which lightens humanity, and smiles away the fretting thoughts of care and suffering.

We have turned aside from more practical studies to consider a subject which the utilitarian may regard as of very little use; yet we do not undervalue those studies which are necessary for the free development and complete training of the human mind. But for the mind to be healthy and strong, for it to reach the utmost perfection compatible with its nature, it must have recreation, even in its studies. A wise and eminently practical man has said, "Cultivate, not only the *corn-fields* of your mind, but the *pleasure-gardens* also." To do this, we cannot do better than to cultivate the capacity for wit and humour, and keep open the natural resources of the mind to all their social and humanizing influences; and we shall soon discover that those movements of the mind which we generalize under the names of wit and humour, are not merely sportive, but that they are also closely allied to the deepest feelings and strongest passions of our nature, and form part and parcel of the world's literature and life.

CHARLES DICKENS.

"The good, the gentle, high-gifted, ever-friendly, noble Dickens—every inch of him an honest man."—*Thomas Carlyle.*

CHARLES DICKENS.

However much we may call this an unromantic age, an age of utility, logic, and science, yet imagination plays now as an important part in human affairs as it ever has done. By imagination we mean that creative power, or call it by whatsoever name you may, which is the element of every great mind; that grand poetic faculty which inspires the mighty artist, poet, or novelist, and which pours out its creative energy upon the sublimest works of philosophy and history. The works of imagination have outlived, and they are likely to outlast, all the other works of man. Our earliest historical traditions are preserved in poetry, and it is poetry which has made history imperishable. "The philosophy of history," it has been well said, "may be denominated the philosophy of romance." In our own literature how large a portion of poetry and fiction has been preserved in every age! This will always be so, for the human heart is ever the same in every generation: it aspires after something better than the events of our common life, and craves for more satisfaction than the world can give. The poet and novelist, in their reflections and transfigurations of human life, with all its pageantries, its fortunes, its passions, its greatness and littleness, will ever be interesting to us. Truth makes fiction, for the novelist idealizes the real. He does not make a world, but uses the materials he finds in it. Nothing human is indifferent to him. He sees life on all sides—its tragedy and comedy, its laughter and tears—and his excellency mainly consists in the breadth and width of his sympathies in the comprehensiveness and versatility of his conceptions.

One of the greatest of our modern novelists for creative power, imagination, wit, and humour, combined with wide-ranging sympathies (for his heart is more comprehensive than his understanding) — the novelist who is, perhaps, dearer to us than any other, and one of the names in this age we are most proud of (we do not say that it is the greatest, but we love it the most) is the subject of our study — Charles Dickens. When we think of the hearths he has brightened, the homes he has cheered, the hearts he has gladdened, the laughter and tears he has evoked, the charity and love he has infused into our nature, we feel that it is these God-gifted children who have made this world not only habitable, but enjoyable for us. One of the secrets of Dickens' success was that he knew something of the human heart, "its tricks and manners;" that he could move us to laughter or tears at the commonest things. If he could not sound the depth or tumult of the soul, he could touch those lighter feelings which play upon the surface of our nature, and which are common to us all. He could write first-rate nonsense—a gift which is not to be despised, for nonsense is the very essence of mirth. If we laugh heartily, we cannot often give a *reason* for our doing so, and we all know how dismal and hopeless a task it is to *explain* a joke. What a host of sportive beings thronging and crowding into the brain he has conjured up, " unwearied in rogueries, and drolleries, and wheedling gibes, and loud, ringing, extravagant laughter!" In this world it is but little some of us can find to laugh at. The consequence is that one of God's best gifts to man is sorely neglected. But a wise and beneficent Power has given us more occasions for laughter than for tears. For, says the poet, " In Nature there is nothing melancholy"; therefore, let us be thankful to the man who can lead us into the realms of fun and nonsense, who can make us laugh at our own absurdities as well as those of other people. Dickens' early works are brimful of genuine English laughter—" a laughter holding both its sides." Gifted originally with a joyous temperament, great animal spirits, and a keen sense of the ludicrous, he has been enabled to show us the fun, frolic, and sunny side of human life; yet he does not forget the *uses* of laughter. He has laughed down abuses where crying and preaching had been of little avail. If some of his characters are not lovable, they are at least laughable; if we cannot always laugh *with* them, he can make us laugh *at* them; but it is a laughter in which there is no malice—which tickles, but leaves no sting behind. " If," he wrote, in one of his early prefaces, " he should only induce one reader to think better of his fellow men, and to look upon the brighter and more kindly side of human nature, he would indeed be proud and happy to have led to such a result." And again, in reviewing his past efforts, he once said, "I felt an earnest and humble desire, and shall do till I die, to increase the stock of harmless cheerfulness. I felt that the world was not utterly to be despised; that it was worthy of living in for many reasons."

But it is not for laughter only that we prize our author; shall we not bless him also for the tears he has evoked? He has caused us to shed tears of love for those who have departed—those long-buried, beauteous forms, upon whom "the mossy marbles rest," and fond memory has "cleansed from the dishonours of the grave." Many a mother has wept afresh "a fountain of sweet tears" for her lost darling over the grave of "Little Nell." Many a man bowed in sorrow, whose heart's fountain has been long dry in the barrenness of busy life, has wept afresh in remembrance of "Paul Dombey." We feel that such tears are not maudlin, for they make the heart better. They are not like the whinings and whimperings of a false sensibility, which laughs and weeps for mere entertainment over the pages of the last new novel, leaving the reader often in a state of mental intoxication, sometimes under the mild stimulus of pap, though, to suit the palate of the regular literary dram-drinker, it is necessary to make the mixture strong—to

"Banish sense and wit,
And dash in lots of madness."

Dickens loved the creations of his own imagination;

they were dear as his own children, and like flesh and blood to him. We read in his life how all these sportive beings were alive in his fancy, and such was their intense individuality, that "every word said by his characters. he confessed to G. H. Lewes, was distinctly heard by him." Thus he did not use his imagination so much as his imagination used him. If any of his characters are inspired with life, they first of all inspired him, for he laughed and wept with them, and seemed as much under their influence as Goethe, when he said, "I feel myself surrounded, nay besieged, by all the spirits I ever conjured up." In a letter to Forster, his biographer, written in a time of illness and sorrow, he says, "But may I not be forgiven for thinking it a wonderful testimony of my being made for my art, that when, in the midst of this trouble and pain, I sit down to my book, some beneficent power shows it all to me, and tempts me to be interested? and I don't invent it—really do not—but *see* it, and write it down." Yet his characters are not mere abstractions spun out of his brain: they carry the air of the world, and not the close atmosphere of the study about with them. We know them the moment we meet them, for they are like living beings: "they speak like men, not like authors." In the street and market, in church and chapel, in society and in the family, we meet, rub shoulders, and recognise the Pecksniffs, Micawbers, Swivellers, and the Nicklebys, &c. They are not caricatures, for a caricaturist rarely presents but a bare outline or grotesque exaggeration of some peculiarity which marks the man, without representing him; while Dickens presents the man, the actual features and lineaments, though exaggerated in small details, yet perfect as a whole. We feel that it is almost impossible to believe that such persons as Mrs. Gamp, Mr. Micawber, Pecksniff, or the Wellers, never had an existence, and this belief was shared by none more than by Dickens himself. Alexander Smith says in one of his essays, "If Mr. Dickens' characters were gathered together, they would constitute a town populous enough to send a representative to Parliament. Let us enter. The style of architecture is unparalleled. There is an individuality about the buildings. In some obscure way they remind one of human faces. There are houses sly-looking, houses wicked-looking, houses pompous-looking. Heaven bless us! what a rakish pump! What a self-important town-hall! What a hard-hearted prison! The dead walls are covered with advertisements of Mr. Sleary's circus. Newman Noggs comes shambling along. Mr. and the Misses Pecksniff come sailing down the sunny side of the street. Miss Mercy's parasol is gay; papa's neckcloth is white and terribly starched. Dick Swiveller leans against a wall, his hands in his pockets, a primrose held between his teeth, contemplating the opera of Punch and Judy, which is being conducted under the management of Messrs. Codlin and Short. You turn a corner, and you meet the coffin of little Paul Dombey borne along. Who would have thought of encountering a funeral in this place? In the afternoon you hear the rich tones of the organ from Miss La Creevy's first floor for Tom Pinch has gone to live there now, and you know all the people as you know your own brothers and sisters, and consequently require no letters of introduction, you go up and talk with the dear old fellow about all his friends and your friends, and towards evening he takes your arm, and you walk out to see poor Nelly's grave— a place which he visits often, and which he dresses with his own hands."

Some of Dickens' characters are stereotyped in a few words. Read the account of the pleasant little family circle assembled in Pecksniff's best parlour in expectation of old Martin Chuzzlewit's death as an illustration of Dickens' power of sketching character by a few graphic verbal combinations. "But when the company arrived! That was the time. When Mr. Pecksniff, rising from his seat at the table's head, with a daughter on either hand, received his guests in the best parlour, and motioned them to chairs, with eyes so overflowing, and countenance so damp with gracious perspiration, that he may be said to have been in a kind of moist meekness! And the company, the jealous, stony-hearted, distrustful company, who were all shut up in themselves, and had no faith in anybody, and wouldn't believe anything, and would no more allow themselves to be softened or lulled asleep by the Pecksniffs than if they had been so many hedgehogs or porcupines. First there was Mr. Spottletoe, who was so bald, and had such big whiskers, that he seemed to have stopped his hair, by the sudden application of some powerful remedy, in the very act of falling off his head, and to have fastened it irrevocably on his face. Then there was Mrs. Spottletoe, who, being much too slim for her years, and of a poetical constitution, was accustomed to inform her more intimate friends that the said whiskers were 'the lodestar of her existence,' and who could now, by reason of her strong affection for her uncle Chuzzlewit, and the shock it gave her to be suspected

of testamentary designs upon him, do nothing but cry—
except moan. Then there were Anthony Chuzzlewit and
his son Jonas. The face of the old man, so sharpened by
the wariness and cunning of his life that it seemed to cut
him a passage through the crowded room as he edged
away behind the remotest chairs, while the son had so well
profited by the precept and example of the father, that he
looked a year or two the elder of the twain, as they stood,
winking their red eyes, side by side, and whispering to
each other, softly. Then there was the widow of a deceased
brother of Martin Chuzzlewit, who, being almost super-
naturally disagreeable, and having a dreary face, and a bony
figure, and a masculine voice, was, in right of these qualities,
what is commonly called a strong-minded woman; and
who, if she could, would have established her claim to the
title, and have shown herself, mentally speaking, a perfect
Samson, by shutting up her brother-in-law in a private
madhouse until he proved his complete sanity by loving
her very much. Beside her sat her spinster daughters, three
in number, and of gentlemanly deportment, who had so
mortified themselves with tight stays, that their tempers
were reduced to something less than their waists, and sharp
lacing was expressed in their very noses. Then there was
a young gentleman, grand-nephew of Mr. Martin Chuzzlewit, very dark and very hairy, and apparently born for no
particular purpose but to save looking-glasses the trouble
of reflecting more than just the first idea and sketchy
notion of a face which had never been carried out. Then
there was a solitary female cousin, who was remarkable for
nothing but being very deaf, and living by herself, and
always having the tooth-ache. Then there was George

Chuzzlewit, a gay bachelor cousin, who claimed to be young, but had been younger, and was inclined to corpulency, and rather overfed himself, to that extent, indeed, that his eyes were strained in their sockets, as if with constant surprise; and he had such an obvious disposition to pimples, that the bright spots on his cravat, the rich pattern on his waistcoat, and even his glittering trinkets, seemed to have broken out upon him, and not to have come into existence comfortably. Last of all there were present Mr. Chevy Slyme and his friend Tigg. And it is worthy of remark that although each person present disliked the other, mainly because he or she did belong to the family, they one and all concurred in hating Mr. Tigg because he didn't."

The whole account of the meeting of this family of hedgehogs is very amusing. If Dickens has painted the best and brightest side of human nature, he has portrayed the worst and darkest side also. His villains are of nearly every type, and they are like Mephistopheles—real, walking, every-day, flesh-and-blood devils. Dickens did not create them, but found them in every grade of society, and painted them. Villains are unfortunately part and parcel of the world, and

"We must not wink and shut our apprehensions up
From common sense of what men were and are."

The novelist would be untrue to nature and the world if he did not represent and expose meanness, deformity, and vice in all its forms. But Dickens does not attempt to make bad good or good bad, as some novelists have done. If he has depicted the religious hypocrite, it was not for want of reverence for true religion, but because the religious devil is the worst of all devils. "I have always striven," he says, in one of his letters, "to express veneration in my writings for the life and lessons of our Saviour, because I feel it." He does not make a sweet electuary of vice to give a zest and wicked relish to excess, or attempt to startle and make a sensation by descending the depths of pandemonium for originalities of diabolism, and by extolling the virtues of the vicious give to infamy a kind of fame, or by the licentiousness of a fervent imagination endeavour to transform the foul crime of the seducer, the adulterer, and the assassin into a dainty work of art. He sees "some soul of goodness in things evil," and his keen sense of the ludicrous often modifies his sensibility of what is detestable so as to change the deformed into the grotesque. If he introduces into some of his worst characters the humour and foibles of our better nature, it is to prevent us from degenerating into "the heart poison of contempt and hatred," that we may pity more than we despise them. How unconsciously some of his villains play their deep game of hypocrisy, pretending not to detect or know each other's schemes, and to deceive each other by using the language of virtue and affection. This sense of incongruity lies often at the root of Dickens' humour. When Snawley tries to kidnap poor Smike by claiming him as his own son, he indulges in a strain of snivelling eloquence upon the beauty of natural affection—"the elevated feeling, the feeling of the ancient Romans and Grecians, and of the beasts of the field, and birds of the air, with the exception of rabbits and tom-cats, which sometimes devour their offspring. My heart yearned towards him. I could have—I don't know what I couldn't have done to him in the anger of a father." "It only shows what natur' is, sir," said Mr. Squeers. "She's a rum'un is natur'." "She is a holy thing, sir," remarked Snawley. "I believe you," added Mr. Squeers, with a moral sigh; "I should like to know how we could ever get on without her! Natur'," said Mr. Squeers solemnly, "is more easier conceived than described. Oh! what a blessed thing, sir, to be in a state of natur'."

Quilp, in the *Old Curiosity Shop*, is a toadlike lump of limb and feature, a villain of monkeylike mischievousness, combined with demonlike malice. He represents one of the worst traits in human nature that it is capable of—"motiveless malignity." His coadjutor is Sampson Brass, a pettifogging attorney. When Quilp employs him to entrap Kit Nubbles in a theft, by placing a bank-note in the boy's hat, upon the discovery of the supposed robbery Brass clasped his hands, and exclaimed, with an ejaculation of horror, "And this is the world that turns upon its own axis, and has lunar influences, and revolutions round heavenly bodies, and various games of that sort! This is human natur', is it? Oh, natur'! natur'!" It is in these conceits and oddities of expression, in the quaint contact of the comic with the solemn, the like with the unlike, and the grotesque exaggeration of the common and the familiar, which gives us an interest and a laughing toleration for what would otherwise be commonplace. A few instances will suffice as illustrations.

When Ralph Nickleby says "God bless you!" to his niece, "the blessing seemed to stick in his throat, as if it were not used to the thoroughfare, and didn't know the way out." When Squeer's son catches poor Smike, his father, after praising his sharpness, gives him this advice: "You always keep on in the same path, and do them things that you see your father do, and when you die you'll go right slap to heaven, and no questions asked." Mr. Squeer's description of his injuries, received from Nicholas Nickleby, is another instance of Dickens' own peculiar humour. "I was one blessed bruise, sir," said Squeers, touching first the roots of his hair, and then the toes of his boots, 'from *here* to *there*.' Vinegar and brown paper—vinegar and brown paper from morning to night. I suppose there was a matter of half a ream of brown paper stuck upon me from first to last. As I laid all of a heap in our kitchen, plastered all over, you might have thought I was a large brown paper parcel, chock full of nothing but groans."

In *Pickwick* there is more fun and frolic than in any other single book of Dickens, or perhaps any other author. It is inflated with the laughing-gas of wit and humour. From beginning to end the "mirth is fast and furious." After reading it one may measure his capacity for laughter ever afterwards. It is a comedy, presenting a series of shifting scenes — now in the country, now in the town, in the farmhouse, or in streets, gardens, law courts, offices, and hotels—one humorous adventure following another in rapid succession, interspersed with comic scenes and startling surprises, yet connected with scarcely any plot. Every page is alive with character; and what variety is there! The immortal Samuel Pickwick, a worthy descendant of Falstaff, in that he is the most humorous creation of the age; the timid, sporting Mr. Winkle, the susceptible Tupman, the poetic Snodgrass, the bluff, hearty Wardle, the lugubrious rascal Job Trotter, the loquacious Jingle, the hysterical Mrs. Bardell, the two Wellers, and the fat boy, with a variety of others, all interesting, moving and jostling each other through the novel. The wit of Weller and son is of the streets streety, and it is a boast of old Weller that he gave a good street education to his son. When Pickwick expresses himself satisfied with Sam: "Wery glad to hear it, sir," replied the old man. "I took a great deal o' pains with his eddication, sir; let him run in the streets when he was wery young and shift for hisself. It's the only way to make a boy sharp, sir." The Wellers were not romantic characters (and to the superfine inanities of affected gentility they may be considered vulgar), but they represented a phase of life which was comparatively unknown to us. The elder Weller's eccentricities are mostly expressed in his aversions. He had married a widow, or rather, a widow had married him, and one of the blessings of his connubiality is that he found it a sovereign cure for an old complaint, the seat of which is a long way from the heart, viz., the gout, and he gives the following prescription to Mr. Pickwick:—"The gout, sir, is a complaint as arises from too much ease and comfort. If ever you're attacked with the gout, sir, just you marry a widder as has got a good loud voice, with a decent notion of usin' it, and you'll never have the gout agin. It's a capital prescription, sir. I takes it reg'lar, and I can warrant it to drive away any illness as is caused by too much jollity." The elder Weller's personality is never forgotten; his rosy, blossoming face, the result of fresh air and potations; his round, fat body, like Falstaff, stuffed full of conceits and humours, breaking out now and then in a paroxysm of chuckles and half-choking, suppressed laughter at his own jests and waggeries; he has perfect faith in his own infallible wisdom, which manifests itself in all the oddities of self-assertion, as between the whiffs of his pipe and the winks of his eye he delivers his oracular sayings, with all the air of a knowing one, or with a sigh of self-abashment as he feels that he is a deluded victim, when he utters his opinions upon matrimony and widows. The old man's horror when he sees his son Sam writing a valentine (the description of which is as natural as a picture of W. Hunt's) is thus very characteristically expressed:—" To see you married, Sammy, to see you a deluded wictim, and thinkin' in your innocence it's all wery capital. It is a dreadful trial to a father's feelings, that 'ere, Sammy." In the two Wellers, Dickens has shown, what he is constantly endeavouring to teach us, that in what is called vulgar life there are all those qualities, good and evil, the same virtues and vices, which are found in every grade of society, and that they are inseparable from our common humanity. "There is never vulgarity," says Ruskin, "in a whole truth, however commonplace. It may be unimportant or painful: it cannot be vulgar. Vulgarity is only in concealment of truth, or in affectation."

It is to be hoped that in these days of growing distrust between the employer and the employed, the old feelings of attachment which Sam Weller felt and expressed towards his master will not be difficult a few generations hence to understand, so that the following passage will need a commentator (except for the cockneyisms): "If you vant a more polished sort of feller, vell and good—have him; but vages or no vages, notice or no notice, board or no board, lodgin' or no lodgin', Sam Veller, as you took from the old inn in the Borough, sticks by you come what come may, and let ev'rythin' and ev'rybody do their wery fiercest, nothing shall ever perwent it." It is remarkable that, overflowing as Pickwick is with wit and humour, we never feel that it is overdone. The mind does not tire, nor the interest flag from beginning to end. We do not, as in some professedly witty books, read, laugh, and yawn from a wearied sense of the ludicrous. We feel that we are in contact with a youthful, healthy genius, rioting in the full play of fresh animal spirits, the influence of which is more or less communicated to us.

Taking individual characters and analyzing them, we find how much Dickens has drawn upon himself and the world in his representations of men by close observation of their actions. Perhaps few authors have been less dependent upon books. We can trace the influence of Goldsmith, Fielding, and Washington Irving in some of his characters, but it is more an objective than a subjective resemblance. Selecting three or four of his characters as examples of his genius, we present them as Dickens', and as his only. Without any chronological order we take Mr. Pecksniff first as a representative of sublime hypocrisy. A French critic, M. Henri Taine, selects him as a familiar type of the English mind. Some of the observations upon his character will most likely be amusing to our readers. "The first fruits of English society," says he, " is hypocrisy. It ripens under the double breath of religion and morality. He confesses that as the Frenchman has no religion he has no occasion for hypocrisy. The vice is therefore English. Mr. Pecksniff is not found in France. If the French have an affectation it is not of virtue but of vice. They had their hypocrites once, but it was when religion was popular; since Voltaire, Tartuffe is impossible." M. Taine's rhetoric is better than his logic. The hypocrite is just as detestable when he affects vice as when he affects virtue, and pays court to falsehood instead of truth. "Hypocrisy is a compliment which vice pays to virtue." If there were no virtue there would be no vice, if no truth no falsehood; as, if there were no genuine coin, there would be no counterfeit. M. Taine pays this unconscious compliment to his own nation, that it has neither religion, truth, nor virtue. He spurts forth his venom against the wind, which blows back in his own face.

Mr. Pecksniff is one of those moral rascals "whose soul is a rank poison thorough"—one who preaches morality without practising it, and who is "fuller of virtuous precepts than a copybook." He is a Cheap Jack philanthropist, whose sentiments are his wares, who sells brass for gold, and tin for silver. Like many other immoral rascals, he finds a moral in everything. Thus, after his stomach is well charged, he seasons his meal with a moral; and even cream, sugar, tea, toast, ham and eggs, are the subjects of his serene platitudes. "The process of digestion," says he, "as I have been informed by anatomical friends, is one of the most wonderful works of nature. I do not know how it may be with others, but it is a great satisfaction to me to know, when regaling on my humble fare, that I am putting in motion the most beautiful machinery with which we have any acquaintance. I really feel at such times as if I was doing a public service when I have wound myself up, if I may employ such a term," said Mr. Pecksniff, with exquisite tenderness, "and know that I am going. I feel that in the lesson afforded by the works within me I am a benefactor to my kind!" Mr. Pecksniff is moral in his drunkenness, and cants even in his disgrace and discovery. When his friends carry him up to bed in a state of intoxication, he endeavours to improve the occasion by appearing strangely attired on the landing, calling to those below, " My friends, let us improve our minds by mutual inquiry and discussion. Let us be moral. Let us contemplate existence." In his family the hoof constantly shows itself beneath the angel's robe, and he "carries stings even in his tears," for the greater the villany he is going to perpetrate the more is his affectation of virtue.

Let us look at another personage—Miss Miggs, in *Barnaby Rudge*. She may be taken as a representative of one of those social malignants who are the pest of a household, whose breath is a moral poison, drawing nourishment from defamings. As half-servant and half-companion she uses her influence by craft, slander, and malice, to make a whole family miserable. Miss Miggs, " or as she was called in conformity with those prejudices of society which lop and top from poor handmaidens all such genteel excrescences, Miggs"—this Miggs was a lady of uncertain age and uncertain temper, with a long, lean, and rather uncomfortable figure, and of a style of beauty Sim Tappertit described as "scraggy." She was an heroic virgin, with a tendency to hysterics. Miggs had a spontaneous aversion to the human kind in general, and to *man*kind in particular. "The latter she held to be fickle, false, base, sottish, inclined to perjury, and wholly undeserving. And she was accustomed to wish that the whole race of woman could but die off in order that the men might be brought to know the real value of the blessings by which they set so little store. Nay, her feeling for her order ran so high that she sometimes, declared, if she could only have good security for a fair round number—say ten thousand—of young virgins following her example, she would, to spite mankind, hang, drown, stab, or poison herself with a joy past all expression." When she watches at the window for the return of Sim Tappertit in order to betray him, she is described as "having an expression of face in which a great number of opposite ingredients, such as mischief, cunning, malice, triumph, and patient expectation, were all mixed up together in a kind of physiognomical punch," and as composing herself to wait and listen, "like some fair ogress who has set a trap, and was waiting for a nibble from a plump young traveller." Miggs is an example of the misery that can be inflicted by beings the most insignificant and contemptible, and by none more than through the petty meanness and cunning weakness of an unfeminine woman.

Mrs. Gamp is a figure which is haply one of the past; but at one time these birth and death hunters had the power of inflicting an amount of misery upon the helpless as now makes us shudder. In sketching her character, Dickens has exposed the ignorance and brutality of that class of hired attendant upon the poor as well as the incompetence and cruelty of the hospital nurses of that time through Betsy Prig. Mrs. Gamp is one of the most humorous as well as detestable of his characters. As soon as we are introduced to her in her lodgings in Kingsgate Street, her figure is never forgotten, with her large bundle, pair of pattens, and gig umbrella. Here is her description: "She was a fat old woman, this Mrs. Gamp, with a husky voice and a moist eye, which she had a remarkable power of turning up, and only showing the white of it. Having very little neck, it cost her some trouble to look over herself, if one may say so, at those to whom she talked. She wore a very rusty black gown, rather the worse for snuff, and a shawl and bonnet to correspond. In these dilapidated articles of dress she had on principle arrayed herself, time out of mind, on such occasions as the present, for this at once expressed a decent amount of veneration for the deceased, and invited the next of kin to present her with a fresher suit of weeds —an appeal so frequently successful, that the very fetch and ghost of Mrs. Gamp, bonnet and all, might be seen hanging up, any hour in the day in at least a dozen of the second-hand clothes' shops about Holborn. The face of Mrs. Gamp—the nose in particular—was somewhat red and swollen, and it was difficult to enjoy her society without becoming conscious of a smell of spirits, a peculiar fragrance, which is afterwards described, "as if a passing fairy had hiccoughed, and had previously been to a wine vaults." Like most persons who have attained to great eminence in their profession, she took to hers very kindly; insomuch that, setting aside her natural predilections as a woman, she went to a lying-in or a laying-out with equal zest and relish." Thus we have a picture of the nurse of the past, "coarse, greedy inhuman, jovial, prowling about young wives with a leer, and old men with a look that would fain lay them out, ready at every festivity to put the bottle to her lips, and at every calamity to squat down, and find in it her own account of pickled salmon and cucumber." Dickens has done good service in helping to put this race of vampires out of existence, and now Mrs. Gamp has become as immortal, and, haply, as invisible, as the potential form of her friend Mrs. Harris. This may be the author's justification in expending the best powers of his satire and humour upon so worthless an object, which, if it were not for some good purpose, would otherwise seem "like pouring rosewater over a toad."

Take any of Dickens' principal characters, and we always find the same freshness and originality, as if stamped from Nature's mint. It is of very loose materials that he sometimes makes up his characters. Dick Swiveller is a specimen of a vain, reckless, cracked-brained, cockney-bred, good-natured vagabond, whose mind, like his coat, is made up of "shreds and patches;" scraps of songs, plays, slang, convivial toasts, and sentiments are for ever floating through his helter-skelter brain. Yet out of this conglomeration of vanity and conceit, recklessness and idleness, Dickens finds some good at the bottom, and Dick, after a series of shifting adventures, comes out right at last. Eugene Wrayburn, in *Our Mutual Friend*, is another example of the same class. They are not the ordinary materials for the making of heroes, but they are better than those dummies made up of tailors' stuff which some of our fashionable novelists parade before their readers: the chief merit of the writers consists in their being well skilled in the art of draping the human figure, and who in their profound knowledge of clothes often forget to put men inside them, or the man and the garment are so much alike that we cannot tell one from the other.

One remarkable characteristic of Dickens' writings is his habit of personification, so as to give a human interest to inanimate things, clothing them with the attributes of flesh and blood. He is something like Balzac, who said that he could not describe a landscape until he had turned himself for a time into trees, grass, and flowers, mountains, rivers, and effects of sunlight, &c., so that he became, as it were, part of them, and they part of him. Dickens painted old walls, hulls of boats, tumble-down and rotten houses, ivy-grown and mouldering churches, the scarred ruin, &c., with the loving hand of an artist, as if they were living forms. The winds, streams, and woods are haunted with spirits; the night winds sigh and moan with pain, and hover about like phantoms, giving an almost supernatural terror to darkness. Here is a description, wild and weird, of the night wind wandering round a church, "and moaning as it goes, and trying with its unseen hand, the windows and the doors, and seeking out some crevices by which to enter: and when it has got in, as one not finding what it seeks, whatever that may be, it wails and howls to issue forth again: and, not content with stalking through the aisies, and gliding round and round the pillars, and tempting the deep organ, soars up to the roof, and strives to rend the rafters; then flings itself despairingly upon the stones below, and passes, muttering, into the vaults. Anon, it comes up stealthily, and creeps along the walls, seeming to read, in whispers, the Inscriptions sacred to the Dead. At some of these it breaks out shrilly, as with laughter, and at others, moans and cries as if it were lamenting. It has a ghostly sound too, lingering within the altar, where it seems to chaunt in its wild way of Wrong and Murder done, and false Gods worshipped, in defiance of the Tables of the Law, which look so fair and smooth, but are so flawed and broken. Ugh! Heaven preserve us, sitting snugly round the fire! It has an awful voice, that wind at Midnight, singing in a church!

"But high up in the steeple! There the foul blast roars and whistles! High up in the steeple, where it is free to come and go through many an airy arch and loophole, and to twist and twine itself about the giddy stair, and twirl the groaning weathercock, and make the very tower shake and shiver! High up in the steeple, where the belfry is, and iron rails are ragged with rust, and sheets of lead and copper, shrivelled by the changing weather, crackle and heave beneath the unaccustomed tread; and birds stuff shabby nests into corners of old oaken joists and beams; and dust grows old and grey; and speckled spiders, indolent and fat with long security, swing idly to and fro in the vibration of the bells, and never loose their hold upon their thread-spun castles in the air, or climb up sailor-like in quick alarm, or drop upon the ground, and ply a score of nimble legs to save one life! High up in the steeple of an old church, far above the light and murmur of the town, and far below the flying clouds that shadow it, is the wild and dreary place at night."

A want of condensation is a fault which is often found with Dickens. This may arise in a great measure from his writing his novels in periodical numbers, so that he had often to write against time, and which perhaps caused him sometimes to spin out page after page of wearisome dialogue. He grows tedious also in depicting high life, as if out of his element. His lords are merely stuffed figures. Perhaps he intended them only to be such. "They are ugly all over with affectation," and may be classed with his fops and toadies who lisp and stammer out the double-distilled, brainless twaddle of the drawing-room. But this fault cannot be found with his sketches and smaller stories, and notably among these his *Great Expectations*, *Hard Times*, and *Tale of Two Cities*. His earlier Christmas stories are perfect in form and sharply defined. That of Captain Richard Doubledick among *The Seven Poor Travellers' Tales* is one of the most pathetic in our language. There is also a sketch of one of the passengers on board a steamboat in the *American Notes*, which is a perfect miniature. We give it entire. "There was a little woman on board, with a little baby, and both little woman and little child were cheerful, good-looking, bright-eyed, and fair to see. The little woman had been passing a long time with her sick mother in New York, and had left her home in St. Louis in that condition in which ladies who truly love their lords desire to be. The baby was born in her mother's house, and she had not seen her husband (to whom she was now returning) for twelve months: having left him a month or two after their marriage. Well, to be sure, there never was a little woman so full of hope, and tenderness, and love, and anxiety as this little woman was: and all day long she wondered whether 'He' would be at the wharf, and whether 'He' had got her letter, and whether, if she sent the baby ashore by somebody else, 'He' would know it, meeting it in the street—which, seeing that he had never set eyes upon it in his life, was not very likely in the abstract, but was probable enough to the young mother. She was such an artless little creature, and was in such a sunny, beaming, hopeful state, and let out all this matter clinging close about her heart so freely, that all the other lady passengers entered into the spirit of it as much as she; and the captain (who heard all about it from his wife) was wondrous sly, I promise you, inquiring every time we met at table, as in forgetfulness, whether she expected anybody to meet her at St. Louis, and whether she would want to go ashore the night we reached it (but he supposed she wouldn't), and cutting many other dry jokes of that nature. There was one little, weazen, dried-apple-faced old woman who took occasion to doubt the constancy of husbands in such circumstances of bereavement, and there was another lady (with a lap-dog) old enough to moralize on the lightness of human affections, and yet not so old that she could help nursing the baby, now and then, or laughing with the rest when the little woman called it by its father's name, and asked it all manner of fantastic questions concerning him in the joy of her heart. It was something of a blow to the little woman that when we were within twenty miles of our destination it became clearly necessary to put this baby to bed. But she got over it with the same good humour, tied a handkerchief round her head, and came out into the little gallery with the rest. Then such an oracle as she became in reference to the localities! and such facetiousness as was displayed by the married ladies! and such sympathy as was shown by the single ones! and such peals of laughter as the little woman herself (who would just as soon have cried) greeted every jest with!

"At last there were the lights of St. Louis, and here was the wharf, and those were the steps, and the little woman, covering her face with her hands, and laughing (or seeming to laugh) more than ever, ran into her own cabin, and shut herself up. I have no doubt that in the charming inconsistency of such excitement she stopped her ears lest she should hear 'Him' asking for her; but I did not see her do it. Then a great crowd of people rushed on board, though the boat was not yet made fast, but was wandering about among the other boats to find a landing-place, and everybody looked for the husband, and nobody saw him, when in the midst of us all— Heaven knows how she ever got there—there was the little woman clinging with both arms tight round the neck of a fine, good-looking, sturdy young fellow! and in a moment afterwards there she was again actually clapping her little hands for joy as she dragged him through the small door of her small cabin to look at the baby as he lay asleep!"

Dickens' success was as great in pathos as in humour; his glance was as quick to detect the beautiful as the grotesque and the ludicrous. His perception of moral beauty was as refined as his conceptions were in their finer traits tender and natural—they sprung up in his soul as "effortless as woodland nooks send violets up and paint them blue." What a pure and spiritual creation is Little Nell, in the *Old Curiosity Shop*, who though surrounded by fiendish shapes of evil, her footsteps malignantly dogged by Quilp and his wolfish crew, yet is her innocence untouched! "She glides in light, and takes no shadow from them." In her presence the critic is disarmed, and at her death his judgment is blotted out with tears. The cool, keen, shrewd critic Jeffrey wept bitter tears at her death, and loved and blessed Dickens for making him shed them, and as the tale drew to a close Dickens received heaps of anonymous letters, in female hands, imploring him "not to kill little Nell." Was ever such a tribute paid to an author's genius before?

Two passages we cannot help quoting from this novel, but they must necessarily lose much of their effect in being taken from the context; yet, even standing alone, they are perhaps unequalled for their simplicity and poetic beauty. They both refer to the death of little Nell.

"Waving them off with his hand, and calling softly to her as he went, he stole into the room. They who were left behind drew close together, and after a few whispered words—not unbroken by emotion, or easily uttered—followed him. They moved so gently that their footsteps made no noise; but there were sobs from among the group, and sounds of grief and mourning.

"For she was dead. There, upon her little bed, she lay at rest. The solemn stillness was no marvel now.

"She was dead. No sleep so beautiful and calm, so free from trace of pain, so fair to look upon. She seemed a creature fresh from the hand of God, and waiting for the breath of life; not one who had lived and suffered death.

"Her couch was dressed with here and there some winter berries and green leaves, gathered in a spot she had been used to favour. 'When I die, put near me something that has loved the light, and had the sky above it always.' Those were her words.

"She was dead. Dear, gentle, patient, noble Nell was dead. Her little bird—a poor, slight thing, the pressure of a finger would have crushed—was stirring nimbly in its cage; and the strong heart of its child-mistress was mute and motionless for ever.

"Where were the traces of her early cares, her sufferings and fatigues? All gone. Sorrow was dead indeed in her, but peace and perfect happiness were born—imaged in her tranquil beauty and profound repose.

"And still her former self lay there, unaltered in this change. Yes. The old fireside had smiled upon that same sweet face; it had passed, like a dream, through haunts of misery and care; at the door of the poor schoolmaster on the summer evening, before the furnace-fire upon the cold, wet night, at the still bed-side of the dying boy, there had been the same mild lovely look. So shall we know the angels in their majesty after death.

"The old man held one languid arm in his, and had the small hand tight folded to his breast, for warmth. It was the hand she had stretched out to him with her last smile—the hand that had led him on, through all their wanderings. Ever and anon he pressed it to his lips; then hugged it to his breast again, murmuring that it was warmer now; and, as he said it, he looked, in agony, to those who stood around, as if imploring them to help her.

"She was dead, and past all help, or need of it. The ancient rooms she had seemed to fill with life, even while her own was waning fast—the garden she had tended—the eyes she had gladdened—the noiseless haunts of many a thoughtful hour—the paths she had trodden as it were but yesterday—could know her never more.

"'It is not,' said the schoolmaster, as he bent down to kiss her on the cheek, and gave his tears free vent, 'it is not on earth that Heaven's justice ends. Think what earth is, compared with the world to which her young spirit has winged its early flight; and say, if one deliberate wish expressed in solemn terms above this bed could call her back to life, which of us would utter it!'"

The other passage has been transposed by a poet* into irregular verse, and, without any alteration except in the division of lines stands thus:

> "Oh! it is hard to take to heart
> The lesson that such deaths will teach
> But let no man reject it,
> For it is one that all must learn,
> And is a mighty universal truth.

---

* R. H. Horne.

> When death strikes down the innocent and young,
> For every fragile form from which he lets
>   The panting spirit free,
>   A hundred virtues rise,
> In shapes of mercy, charity and love,
> To walk the world and bless it.
>   Of every tear
> That sorrowing mortals shed on such green graves
> Some good is born, some gentler nature comes."

Much might be said of Dickens' tragic power, his delineation of the darker passions of hatred, jealousy, avarice, revenge, despair, and remorse, with all their attendant crimes and follies. Who has so depicted the dismayed and conscience-stricken murderer, his soul hunted and lashed by the avenging furies, the eternal wakefulness of his fevered brain, the torment of unceasing restlessness, the thousand dreadful eyes which peer at him, and the thousand voices which hoot at him from morn till night, from night till morn, through streets and highways, in solitude and in the crowd? His longing to die, yet fear of death, the animal instinct of self-preservation which struggles in vain to escape the swift retribution at his heels. It is marvellous how Dickens has, in the case of the murderer Jonas, for instance, torn open the heart of the poor blood-stained wretch, nestled into his brain, searched his inmost soul, and by laying bare the agony and remorse of his avenging conscience has chilled our life-blood through and through, and taught the woe, unutterable woe, of him "who spills life's sacred stream." According to the ancients, the grand idea of tragedy is the imitation of serious action, employing pity and terror for the purpose of chastening such passions. Dickens never lost sight of this truth in his teaching, for he infused a moral purpose into his vilest conceptions of human character, and he ever strove to make vice hideous and abominable.

If we look at what Dickens by his writings has helped to accomplish, we must place him in the front rank of social reformers; the influence of his early works have re-acted for good upon the national mind. What abuses has he helped to sweep away! How many a nook and corner of the world has he made brighter and happier? What was bad he strove to make good, and what was good he took pains to improve by love, charity, and good humour. Truly he left the world better than he found it, and had the satisfaction to know that he contributed no inconsiderable share in the making it so. The Fleet and Marshalsea Prisons are now swept away, and imprisonment for debt abolished. The Court of Chancery is improved. The reproach and shame of the Yorkshire Schools live only in the memory of "Nicholas Nickleby," and would that we could say the same of our workhouse system, which, according to recent reports, have still quite as easy a way of getting rid of children as they had in "Oliver Twist's" time. There are still to be seen, as Dickens depicted the outside of Whitechapel Workhouse, those figures "withered from a likeness of aught human," those blind, idiotic, diseased, and drunken shapes which are the puzzle and despair of the moralist and philanthropist. Well might Dickens describe them as "those dumb, wet, silent horrors, sphynxes set up against that dark wall, and no one likely to be at the pains of solving them until the general overthrow." What Hercules shall cleanse this foul Augean Stable, and free us from these monsters bred in the filth and slime of our social corruption? No one saw and felt these horrors more clearly and acutely than Dickens; but they did not inspire him with a sceptical distrust of human nature, nor produce the morbid vitality of a despondent humour, so as to darkly bewilder his mind with the confounding paradoxes of human existence. He was more an artist than a moralist. His aim was to paint men as they are, and not as he would wish them to be; and whatever might have been his feelings, he never sacrificed his art by any antagonistic individuality, or by an impertinent intrusion either of his indignation or approval. Yet strong were the ties which bound him to his fellow men, and his life bears more traces than his writings show how he felt himself linked by identity of nature and destiny, yea, by all that unite us under the common name of man, to those poor, unhealthy, degraded, mutilated beings which he saw around him; and it was his humour, and the wit and brightness which God gave him—that saved him from perpetual despair, and through the pilgrimage of this life helped to "charm his pained steps over the burning marl."

It has been objected that Dickens sometimes carried this quality of humour to excess, and overstepped the modesties of art. Dickens felt this, and he owned that it cost him some effort to check the lighter impulses of his heart, and to control its tendency to exuberant and riotous fun. In one of his letters to Lord Lytton, he said, "I work slowly and with great care, and never give way to my invention recklessly, but constantly restrain it, and that I think it is my infirmity to fancy or perceive relations in things which are not apparent generally. Also, I have such an inexpressible enjoyment of what I see in a droll light, that I dare say I pet it as if it were a spoilt child." It may be said in plea of Dickens that it was an excess of nature that sometimes overstepped the modesties of art, and it is this exuberance of nature (a boundless wealth and prodigality of mind, and an extravagant license of fancy) which is perhaps more remarkable in Shakespeare than in any other writer; at times his imagination seems to be "lord of misrule," and the wit and humour of his fools are

"Owned, without dispute,
Throughout the realms of nonsense absolute."

Thus, by the mastery of his uncontrollable genius, he often confounded all rules of art. And here we might add, parenthetically, that there was in Shakespeare's genius an universality which could carry the whole world in his brain, and "clasp the universe to his bosom," and the reason why his heart was strong enough to bear the woes of Hamlet, Othello, and Lear, was because it was large enough to expand to the humours of Falstaff, and to hold the fairy revels of the "Midsummer Night's Dream." He was, indeed, "not one but all mankind's epitome." In these days of ultra-refinement, what prodigies of vanity, self-conceit, and affectation are brought forth now and then. Literary dandies, whom one would never suspect of the infirmity of thinking, and who, by a gratuitous assumption of superiority to everything natural and unaffected, remind us of the coxcomb in Coleman's comedy, when he addresses a blooming country maiden: "Nature is very clever, for she made you; but Nature never could have made me."

As the poet sees everything through "a kind of glory," so the humorist sees life in its varied aspects in the sunshine of his warm, genial spirit. Dickens' humour coloured, more or less, the whole of his writings; not only were external objects reflected in his mind, but his mind was reflected in them as well. He held the mirror up to nature, but the mirror was his own soul, which reflected back, "like the flashing of a shield," its brightness upon everything around him.

It is customary to compare one writer with another, and to show points of resemblance and contrast. In comparing Dickens with the novelists of his own time, the future only will show whether his works will live as long or longer than any of his contemporaries,

"Whose honours with increase of ages grow,
As streams roll down, enlarging as they flow."

It is the fate of most popular novels to pass away with the hour that brought them forth. Opinions, habits of thought, and manners change, and the continual activity of the human mind is such that there is a constant competition to present something new to replace the old. If novels are written for amusement, and generally this is their paramount purpose, they speak to what is least permanent in human sensibilities. But if the novelist penetrates through the outward varieties of character into the inner life, and, with profound insight into the everlasting principles which govern human conduct, depicts the passions and analyses the secret springs of action, he will paint men not only as they are *now*, but as they will *ever* be, as long as the heart remains the same. The popular writer is often but a shrewd observer: he collects the odd humours and fancies, the fashions and follies, the accidental features of modern life, which are but ephemeral and transient, like his writings. One of the most popular novelists of the last century was Richardson, and his popularity was greater in France than here. Yet how few read Richardson now! If we cannot yet fix Dickens' permanent station in our literature, we may compare him with some of the novelists of the past, although it is difficult to measure him when the standard of taste is so different. In most of the novels of the last century we are repelled by the coarse brutality of the times, and those disgusting scenes which amused our forefathers do not amuse us; if we read them now it is more for critical study, and for the best information we can get as to the general state of society; for in the novel "we see the very web and texture of society as it really exists," but the incidents do not live before us, and too often the sparkle of the wit is gone, and the "faded histrionic masqueraders" pass before us like shadows.

Dickens may not have been so close an observer of manners as Fielding, or have had so profound a knowledge of human nature, or presented with such photographic minuteness pictures of the times he lived in; yet there is a wider range of sympathy, a warmer glow of life, a more intense individuality of character, and a greater refinement of feeling than can be found in that novelist, and which to our thinking will give a longer vitality to his writings. His exaggerations of personal foibles and external peculiarities of appearance, his boisterous fun and good humour, are more like Smollett's, with this advantage, that to find his best things we have not to go to a dunghill and scratch them out. He has none of the laughing, leering merriment, forced conceits, and stage clap-trap of Sterne, that profound master of *double entendre*, and most impiously impure writer in our language; his pathos is as fine, though not so affected, and in tenderness and true sensibility he is indisputably above him. Well might Thackeray, in reviewing those past writers, speaking of their coarse and free manners, say, "I am grateful for the innocent laughter and the sweet, unsullied page which the author of *David Copperfield* gives to my children."

In taking leave of our subject, and in trying to give a general impression which Dickens' works as a whole have left upon us, we feel as if we had just parted with a friend who has been our constant companion for some time— who has taken us into his confidence, and introduced us to the companions of his soul, and to the merry, laughing, tricksy children of his brain. He has cheered us when we have been dull, and "touched the spring of laughter by the side of the spring of tears." He has hung beautiful pictures up in our brain, and bottled up sunshine for us and for others, and we hope will continue to do so for many generations to come. We feel that to Dickens we owe many a good and noble thought, many a hearty laugh, many an hour's amusement to charm away despondency and care; and, moreover, he has given us a wider sympathy, a deeper love, a kindlier spirit of charity and toleration for our fellow men, that has helped to make life more beautiful and sweet; and his memory may be embalmed in our hearts by applying to himself the last words he ever uttered in public, on the death of his friend Mr. Maclise: "Incapable of a sordid or ignoble thought, gallantly sustaining the true dignity of his vocation, no artist, of whatsoever denomination, ever went to his rest leaving a golden memory more pure from dross, or having devoted himself with a truer chivalry to the art goddess whom he worshipped."

THOMAS DE QUINCEY

"Mr. De Quincey was a man whose curious idiosyncrasy and whose influence upon literature will, we are confident, awaken more curiosity with future generations of Englishmen than they do with us to-day. He will, we venture to foretell, stand forth more and more prominently as the decades go by."—*New Quarterly Magazine*, July, 1875.

"But for dreams, that lay mosaic worlds tesselated with flowers and jewels before the blind sleeper, and surround the recumbent living with figures of the dead in the upright attitude of life, the time would be too long before we are allowed to join our brothers, parents, friends; every year we should become more and more painfully sensible of the desolation made around us by death, if sleep—the ante-chamber of the grave—were not hung by dreams with the busts of those who live in the other world."—*Jean Paul Richter.*

THOMAS DE QUINCEY.

THE lives of philosophers, poets, and other literary men, are mostly barren of incident. A life spent in the study is generally a quiet, subjective one. Though the men of thought inspire the men of action, yet it is the latter who reap the fruit from the seeds which the former have silently sown. The world owes an eternal obligation to its thinkers. For what a glorious kingdom such men as Homer, Plato, and Shakespeare have opened for us! They helped to bring the kingdom of literature on the earth, and to make the world habitable. Johnson says truly, "That the chief glory of a nation arises from its authors."

If what we have said is true of the silent lives of most thoughtful men, we can take the subject of our present study as an exception to the general order. Here, at least in one part of De Quincey's life and experience, is there told a tale of strange endurance and sorrow—of temptation, dark and strong—of a struggle, the issue of which was either life or death—of a victory, which crowned its victor, not with laurels, but with thorns, and left him bleeding, maimed, and almost helpless.

It is no easy task to give the characteristics of the many-sided mind of this man. Of his multifarious writings, all are strongly marked with the individuality of the author, and distinguished by the characteristic attractions of depth of scholarship, imagination, wit, and humour. He has written upon almost every conceivable subject, and what is more he has written well. At one time he gives us a little egotistical obtrusion in the shape of autobiography; at another, he is discoursing upon philosophy, and calling up the reverent shades of almost every philosopher under the sun, from Thales to Kant. Now he is erecting logical fortifications in which the gods themselves might take refuge; or he is giving lectures upon political economy. Then taking into consideration "murder as one of the fine arts." Anon, he bursts out into beautiful strains of poetry. Then he is lashing with his critical whip, or roasting before the slow fire of his sarcasm some would-be scholar, philosopher, or poet.

Thus, like a restless lodger constantly shifting his apartments, does he wander from subject to subject, yet he makes himself perfectly at home in each, and what is more his writings are invested with all the charms and graces of the scholar, whose richly stored and well-cultivated mind, whose genial, warm, and sympathetic nature, help to make his readers at home with him also. He is a complete master of the English language, even of its slang; and his writings are characterized by eccentricities of thought and manner. In them are constant jerks and changes, sharp angles, and electric points, running commentaries of foot notes, and bristling scholasticisms. Sometimes his thoughts and sentences flow evenly on, interrupted now and then by some contradiction or paradox, which but break their course to music, "as stones break summer rills;" mixed up here and there, too, are exquisite bits of nonsense. Not many, he says, can write first-rate nonsense. His writings remind us of those quaint fantastic carvings in Gothic architecture, where the imagination of the architect has been allowed to run riot, and in which are strangely blended the sublime and the ridiculous. Grotesque and fanciful shapes, with beautiful devices; faces of cherubims and archangels, side by side with goblin-like forms, and unearthly shapes of monstrous divinities.

There are some who object to the overflow of sportive humour in De Quincey's writings, especially in the higher realms of thought. They think it is sacrilegious, and fit only for the novel and the farce; that a man professing himself a philosopher compromises his dignity by indulging in a joke, and would have him bury the stores of his learning and wisdom in the coffin of cold thought. A century ago there were cold, hard-headed philosophers, who sat apart in solemn state. Such Sydney Smith saw in Edinburgh, and of whom he said, "it required a surgical operation to get a joke into their heads." They had no sympathy with the simple and unphilosophic, the ignorant and uneducated, who could only reason, according to the philosophy of Coran, "that the property of rain was to wet, and fire to burn; that good pasture made fat sheep, and that a great cause of the night is the lack of sun." Feeding themselves upon the dry bones of logical facts, they suffered the warm, hearty, breathing spirit of life to dwindle into miserable dyspepsia. They lacked that secretion of good-humour which we might call the gastric juice of the mind, which assimilates the hardest and crudest experiences of life, and gives to our nature a ruddy stimulating glow of health. The consequence is their writings are not "blood-warm," they had no sympathy with human life, nor that "touch of nature which makes the whole world kin." And most of their works have gone to the bottom of that dead sea of literature, and no diving bell will ever bring them up again.

Not like these men is our philosopher:—

> "The pits of laughter dimple in his cheeks,
> And he is rich with quick bouts of merry
> Argument, and witty sallies quenched
> In laughter sweet."

He has taught us also

> "How charming is divine philosophy,
> Not harsh and crabbed, as dull fools suppose,
> But musical as Apollo's lute,
> And a perpetual feast of nectar'd sweets
> Where no crude surfeit reigns."

In De Quincey's humour there are many singular characteristics. Sometimes it is full of playfulness and tenderness, then again it is radiant with fun and frolic, mounting, like Charles Lamb's, with the sudden motion of a rocket into the highest heaven of outrageous fun and absurdity, chasing syllables with the agility of squirrels bounding among the trees, or a cat pursuing its own tail. Like Bishop Berkeley, who commenced one of his treatises on the virtues of tar-water, and ended it on the immortality of the soul, when he begins a subject, no one can tell what it will include. For—

> "His course is like a stream which runs,
>   With rapid change from rocks to roses,
> It slips from politics to puns,
>   It glides from Mahomet to Moses;
> Beginning with the laws which keep
>   The planets in their radiant courses,
> And ending with some precept deep,
>   For dressing eels or shoeing horses."

We might divide his mind into two hemispheres—the mathematical or abstractive, the imaginative or poetical, which are the opposite poles of the sphere of thought. Whether his subjects are logic, political economy, or criticisms upon the higher forms of poetry, he brings to bear upon them the keen analytic faculty of his brain, piercing into the hidden combination of things; at the same time he illuminates and pours into their depths the light of a vivid imagination, clothing them with beauty and poetic sympathy. As examples of his powers of discernment and discrimination, we would refer to his papers upon Plato, Socrates, and Kant, which are of the highest order of philosophical criticism, and also to his articles upon political economy, pronounced by Mr. M'Culloch to be "unequalled for their brevity, pungency, and force." Now, there is not a more difficult study than the science of Political Economy, requiring as it does the greatest tension of the mind, for it embraces all the multifarious social problems of the time, dealing with the abstract calculations of the mathematician and the ideal laws of the socialist on the one hand, and the concrete facts of the moralist, statesman, and philanthropist on the other; and we think it is a proof of the great powers of De Quincey's mind, that he has mastered this subject, and made it intelligible to the ordinary mind. At times, a soft and almost ethereal light gleams through the surface of his writings, tempering his philosophy and connecting it with the subtle mysteries of the universe and of Divine revelation. In reading his autobiographic sketches, we find that even when a boy he was haunted by shadows, and much given to thought and speculation, especially upon religious matters; building castles in the air, ofttimes the abode of giants, such as good old Bunyan saw in his dreams—huge incarnations of doubt and fear. And no enemies are so hard to conquer as invisible ones. The phantoms of the mind cannot be dispatched with knife or sword; and many men, who have stood firm before cannon and steel, and others also who have defied the contradiction of the world, have trembled like children before the creatures of their imagination. These shadowy recollections and dim visions of life, death, and immortality, which flitted across the golden brain of his childhood, were in after-life transfigured before him in his dreams, with all their awe-inspiring associations of grandeur and terror, and in some of his retrospective glances into his childhood—

"When the breeze of a joyful dawn blew free
In the silken sail of infancy."

He makes us feel—

"The truth the poet sings,
That a sorrow's crown of sorrow is remembering happier things."

But the crowning glory of De Quincey's writings is the overmastering power and splendour of his imaginative faculty which is manifested in its full strength in his dreams. The world has always had its dreamers. Plato, of old, had his dreams, and strange dreams too; the mystics of the middle ages walked in the cloudland and dreamland of their poetic philosophy. Shakespeare's spirit held its carnival in his *Midsummer Night's Dream;* and Milton's sightless orbs, with that vision and faculty divine, saw "beyond the compass of sea and land." Of De Quincey's dreams we might say that they are unique in our literature; to find anything like unto them we must go to the writings of the Germans, who have a dream-literature of their own. But, we think, few have dreamed so vividly and magnificently as De Quincey has done. None, we think, have so dipped their pens in the varied hues of sunshine and gloom, or been able to fix that which is fleeting and transient, so as to record the effects produced by that drug which had such a fascinating nfluence over him. We were reading, some time ago, the efforts of a physician, who was also a poet, to put on record at the earliest moment of regaining consciousness, the thought he should find uppermost in his mind after inhaling a pretty full dose of ether. He says:—" The mighty music of the triumphal march into nothingness reverberated through my brain, and filled me with a sense of infinite possibilities which made me an archangel for the moment. The veil of eternity was lifted. The one great truth which underlies all human experience, and is the key to the mysteries that philosophy has sought in vain to solve, flashed upon me in a sudden revelation! Henceforth all was clear, a few words had lifted my intelligence to the level of the knowledge of the cherubim.

As my natural condition returned, I remembered my resolution, and staggering to my desk, I wrote, in ill-shaped, straggling characters, the all-embracing truth still glimmering in my consciousness. The words were these: '*a strong smell of turpentine prevails throughout.*'" Sir Humphrey Davy's experience after inhaling nitrous-oxide gas is much more satisfactory. With the most intense belief and prophetic manner, he exclaimed to Dr. Kingslake, "Nothing exists but thoughts; the universe is composed of impressions, ideas, pleasures, and pains." Properly to understand De Quincey's dreams, and those associations which formed their dark background, we must narrate some of the leading incidents of his life, taking for our guide his own biography, as recorded in *The Confessions of an English Opium Eater*, which we shall endeavour to do as clearly and briefly as possible.

De Quincey's father, a merchant possessed of some considerable fortune, died when he was very young, and left him under the care of guardians, who sent him early to a large public school, where he distinguished himself for his classical attainments, especially for his knowledge of the Greek language. "That boy," said one of his masters, pointing the attention of a stranger to him, "that boy could harangue an Athenian mob better than you or I could address an English one." Having a quarrel with his guardians, he ran away from school. This one erring step changed the current of his destiny, poisoned the fountains of his peace, and laid the foundation of a lifelong repentance.

After many wanderings and hardships, De Quincey made his way to London, where, as with Dr. Johnson, a real hand-to-hand struggle for life commenced. Somewhere he tells us of the awful solitude of the streets of London to a stranger. How, like a drifted weed upon the ocean, or a stray leaf in autumn, a stranger is borne along by the tide of human beings, through the infinite maze of streets, until he loses all sense of companionship in their utter loneliness and want of sympathy. Upon the strength of his future expectations and claims, he unwisely applied to a money-lender for such resources as would enable him to subsist until he reached his majority. During the "law's delay" his resources were entirely exhausted. For the first two months in London he was houseless, and very seldom slept under a roof. Latterly, however, when colder and more inclement weather came on, for some time, as a nightly asylum from the open air, he slept in the house of one of the lowest class of attorneys, who was an agent of the man he had employed to give him relief during his pecuniary embarrassments. This house, which was large and unfurnished, contained at night one inmate, for the attorney himself slept every night in a different quarter of London, in constant fear of arrest for debt. This one inmate, who was his companion, except a multitude of rats, was a poor, friendless, hunger-bitten child about 14 years of age. With this poor girl he shared the lonely apartments of this large dismal and unfurnished house, sleeping upon the floor, with a bundle of law papers for a pillow, and with no other covering from the inclemency of the weather but a horseman's cloak and some fragments of old household remnants which they managed to scrape together. Here he slept for some time, and almost entirely subsisted upon the fragments of biscuits which the attorney left after his scanty breakfast. During the day he wandered about the streets, treading the hard-hearted, stony streets of London, with hunger like a ravening wolf gnawing his vitals; he would have sunk and died, as Otway and others had before him, but for one of those unfortunates who nightly walk the public streets of our large towns. She, a poor orphan and outcast, who lived upon the wages of her shame, when he laid as dead upon the cold stones near one of the large squares of our great city, ministered to his necessities when all the world had forsaken him, and from her own scanty purse quickly procured for him those stimulants which alone could have saved his life. Shortly after this almost miraculous preservation, in his wanderings he met with a friend of his father's family, who rescued him from this life of misery and distress. His first act was to seek out and reward his benefactress, but some unforseen circumstances prevented them ever meeting again. For her he vainly sought in after years in different visits to London, and looked into myriads of female faces with the hope of again meeting her, that he might communicate to her the authentic message of love and forgiveness, even to a repentant Magdalen.

But we must pass over this touching episode of his life, and proceed to that part of his biography in which he has described the effects of that deadly yet fascinating drug, the influence of which in after-life obtained such a fearful sway over him. During his college career, in one of his visits to London, when suffering from toothache, he was recommended by a friend to try opium as a remedy. He took it, and he says: "In an hour, oh heavens! what a revulsion! what an upheaving, from its lowest depths, of the inner spirit! what an apocalypse of the world within me! That my pains had vanished was now a trifle in my eyes; this negative effect was swallowed up in the immensity of those positive effects which had opened before me—in the abyss of divine enjoyment thus suddenly revealed. Here was a panacea for all human woes; here was the secret of happiness, about which philosophers had disputed for so many ages, at once discovered. Happiness might now be bought for a penny, and carried in the waistcoat pocket; portable ecstacies might be had corked up in a pint bottle; and peace of mind could be sent down in gallons by the mail coach."

Opium, when he was enjoying its pleasures, was to him "a restorer of happiness and joy"; with its potent wand it called up "spirits from the vasty deep," and brought into sunny light the features of long buried beauties and blessed household countenances, cleansed from the "dishonors of the grave." The gates of paradise were opened to his vision, and he beheld the pomp of cities and palaces as were never yet beheld by waking eye unless in the clouds: glory beyond glory ever seen is the architecture of these dreams, he beheld.

> "Fabrics of diamond and of gold,
> With alabaster domes and silver spires,
> And blazing terrace upon terrace, high
> Uplifted: here serene pavilions bright
> In avenues disposed; their towers begirt
> With battlements, that on their restless fronts
> Bore stars—illumination of all gems."

The gorgeous magnificence, the surpassing grandeur, the ethereal beauty, the martial-like array of images and figures clothed in all the pomp of diction, and sparkling in their jewelled drapery, clustered together in these dreams, are unsurpassed by any work of imagination in our language.

But, alas! a change came o'er the spirit of his dreams. He was living upon and enjoying that which was "too bright, too good, for human nature's daily food." Like Sancho, he wanted better bread than could be made from wheat. An attack of illness, first produced by some distressing domestic event, led him to take daily what before he had only taken at intervals, and to increase his dose, so that at one time he took 8000 drops of laudanum, or as much as 320 grains of opium per day; this excess, after a time, brought on those effects he has described in his book under the "Pains of Opium." It was then he bowed down to his dark idol, and all the monstrous phenomena were brought on peculiar to a diseased and morbid state of mind—

> "When all the prodigies that haunt and home
> Within a human bosom were brought
> Marvel by marvel, as to Adam once
> The monsters of the deep, that he might name them."

It was then the dark thoughts of his mind, in the clouds of sorrow and despair, took to themselves phantom shapes, as in mountainous districts, objects in the misty distance appear to the eye gigantic forms of terror to affright. Without any voluntary effort, these phantoms came and went, "lifting with a fearful hand the veil that is woven with night and with terror." "At one time," he says, "a theatre seemed suddenly opened and lighted up within my brain, which presented nightly spectacles of more than earthly splendour." Time and space seemed annihilated.

He says, "I sometimes seemed to have lived for 70 or 100 years in one night; nay, sometimes had feelings representative of a millenium passed in that time, or, however, of a duration far beyond the limits of any human experience." Sometimes the minutest incidents of childhood, or forgotten scenes of later years, were revived; in the twinkling of an eye he saw his whole life reflected as it were in a mirror, showing us that there is no such thing as "forgetting possible to the mind," and that as it has been said at the final judgment, the mind *may* be that dread book of account which the Scriptures speak of, where every thought and incident of our lives are recorded, and which will then be brought to light, when the imperfect veil of memory is drawn aside.

"I feel assured," he says, "that a thousand accidents may and will interpose a veil between our present consciousness and the secret inscriptions on the mind; accidents of the same sort will also rend away this veil; but alike, whether veiled or unveiled, the inscription remains for ever; just as the stars seem to withdraw before the common light of day; whereas, in fact, we all know that it is the light which is drawn over them as a veil, and that they are waiting to be revealed, when the obscuring daylight shall have withdrawn." At another time, in his dreams, History was transfigured before him. In solemn procession passed the actions and deeds of past centuries. Roman pageants and glories, battles, victories, and triumphs, the dry bones of the dead past started into life; cities long since crumbled in the dust were raised again; their streets teemed with busy life; in the market, in the temple, and in the senate chamber, he heard the mighty voices of the past, until, like shadows, they again melted away into the solemn silence of eternity.

> "Then sometime glorious tragedy
> In sceptred pall came sweeping by,
> Presenting Thebes' or Pelop's line,
> Or the tale of Troy divine."

Then came dreams of Oriental imagery, with all the horrors and antipathies of Asiatic life.

He says: "I know not whether others share in my feelings on this point; but I have often thought that if I were compelled to forego England, and to live in China among Chinese manners, and modes of life and scenery, I should go mad. The causes of my horror lie deep, and some of them must be common to others. Southern Asia, in general is the seat of awful images and associations. As the cradle of the human race, if on no other ground, it would have a dim reverential feeling connected with it. The mere antiquity of Asiatic things, of their institutions, histories, above all, of their mythologies, is so impressive, that to me the vast age of the race and name overpowers the sense of youth in the individual. A young Chinese seems to me an antediluvian man renewed. Even an Englishman, though not bred in any knowledge of such institutions, cannot but shudder at the mystic sublimity of castes that have flowed apart, and refused to mix, through such immemorial tracts of time; nor can any man fail to be awed by the sanctity of the Ganges, or by the very name of the Euphrates. In China, over and above what it has in common with the rest of Southern Asia, I am terrified by the modes of life, by the manners, by the barrier of utter abhorrence placed between myself and them, by counter-sympathies deeper than I can analyse. I could sooner live with lunatics, with vermin, with crocodiles or snakes. All this, and much more than I can say, the reader must enter into, before he can comprehend the unimaginable horror which these dreams of Oriental imagery and mythological tortures impressed upon me. Under the connecting feeling of tropical heat and vertical sunlights, I brought together all creatures, birds, beasts, reptiles, all trees and plants, usages and appearances, that are found in all tropical regions, and assembled them together in China or Hindostan. From kindred feelings I soon brought Egypt and her gods under the same law. I was stared at, hooted at, grinned at, chattered at, by monkeys, by paroquets, by cockatoos. I ran into pagodas, and was fixed for centuries at the summit, or in secret rooms; I was the idol! I was the priest! I was worshipped! I was sacrificed! I fled from the wrath of Brama through all the forests of Asia. Vishnu hated me; Seeva lay in wait for me. I came suddenly upon Isis and Osiris; I had done a deed, they said, which the ibis and the crocodile trembled at. Thousands of years I lived, and was buried in stone coffins, with mummies and sphinxes in narrow chambers at the heart of eternal pyramids. I was kissed with cancerous kisses by crocodiles, and was laid confounded with all unutterable slimy things, amongst reeds and Nilotic mud."

De Quincey lived in a dream world, until dreams became as it were the substantial realities of his existence, and by living so long in this abnormal state, he was like the old Dominican friar who shut himself out from the world for years in his cell, with nothing before him but a large picture—so long that he would say, "The world, the world without is a shadow and a dream; but these"—pointing to the figures in the picture—"are realities." Thus De Quincey's waking was like sleeping, and his sleeping like waking, and it became at last impossible to live in either state; and he somewhat resembled the showman's amphibious animal "who cannot live on the land and dies in the water."

> "The miserable power
> To dreams allowed to raise the guilty past,"

was De Quincey's "sorrow's crown of sorrow." The body took revenge upon the soul, and the soul upon the body, and that irresistible imagination, misused and morbidly excited, turned upon its master to rend him. Never did any man more truly realize "the fierce vexation of a dream," or that terrible voice in the incantation of Manfred—

> "Though thy slumber may be deep,
> Yet thy spirit shall not sleep;
> There are shades which will not vanish;
> There are thoughts thou canst not banish.
> . . . .
> And to thee shall night deny
> All the quiet of her sky,
> And the day shall have a sun
> Which shall make thee wish it done."

At last the truth arose in De Quincey's mind, that as he was consuming opium, opium was also consuming *him*, and that the only alternative was either to die in the hands of this monster or to exorcise it. Fearful was the struggle—the struggle of determination against despair. Twice he sank, and twice he rose again; again he sank from ignorance as to the proper remedy.

And here we pause to read the lesson which De Quincey has not been unmindful of teaching us, viz.: of the strength of those habits which will paralyse the strongest man, and in time weave a network around him, galling his very soul, and, like the poisoned shirt of Nessus, by slow degrees consume him.

We cannot enter into details to disclose how De Quincey conquered and laid as it were this monster low, and was able even from its carcass to extract honey and sweetness. Suffice it to say that "he unwound almost to its final links the accursed chain which bound him."

These dreams, which he has described under *The Pleasures and Pains of Opium*, reveal to us the capabilities of infinite pleasure and of infinite pain which exist potentially in the human soul; that "the mind is its own place, and in itself can make a heaven of hell, a hell of heaven." They give us glimpses of that germ of imperishable grandeur which is hidden in our nature, and which reveals itself sometimes through the shattered temple of the soul, sometimes in bodily pain and sickness. As Waller beautifully says—

> "The soul's dark cottage, battered and decayed,
> Let in new lights through chinks which time has made."

These dreams also teach us a fearful lesson as to what exist, and can be brought out from the soul of man to afflict and torment him. Before closing this part of our subject, we notice this remarkable fact, that although De Quincey indulged in opium-eating to a greater excess than has ever been recorded of any other man, and took small quantities until his death, yet he outlived nearly all his contemporaries, and died at a green old age. If opium was a slow poison, it was like the coffee which the young physician denounced before Voltaire under the same name. "You are right there, my friend," said Voltaire; "slow it is, and horribly slow, for I have been drinking it these 70 years, and it has not killed me yet."

It was not by opium-eating alone that De Quincey set at naught the laws of health; his habits were somewhat regular in their irregularity. Thus the Ettrick Shepherd addresses him in the *Noctes Ambrosianæ*. "Mr. De Quinshy, you and me leeves in twa different warlds, and yet it's wonnerfu' hoo we understan' ane anither sae well's we do—quite a phenomena. When I'm soopin, your'e breakfastin'; when I'm lyin' doun, after your coffee your'e risin' up; as I'm coverin' my head wi' the blankets, your'e pittin' on your breeks; as my een are steekin' like sunflowers aneath the moon, your's are glowin' like twa gas lamps; and while your mind is masterin' poleetical economy, and metaphysics in desperate fecht wi' Ricawdro and Cant, I'm heard by the nicht-wanderin' faries snorin' trumpet-nosed through the land o' Nod." At times De Quincey would disappear from his friends for weeks and months together. Dropping in one day to dine with Christopher North, he was detained all night by a storm, and prolonged his impromptu visit for a year. And what a strange visitor he must have been!

But it is not only as a *dreamer* that De Quincey is known. We are not aware of any other author, whether ancient or modern, who has written upon so many subjects

—not even that portentous intellectual Titan, Aristotle—if we were to give an index of his subjects, they might form a library catalogue. The stern utilitarian may despise his dreams and the rich wealth of his imagination, but even he cannot fail to read and admire his treatment of the social and practical questions of the day. Nothing escaped him. Archdeacon Hare called him the greatest logician of our times. His writings may be divided into historical, biographical, critical, political, personal, and miscellaneous. We can only here follow the associations of his life as recorded in his autobiographic sketches, and notice one or two of his papers.

De Quincey lived for a few years at Grasmere, and was on intimate terms with Coleridge, Southey, Wordsworth, Wilson, and others, then living celebrities, of whom he has given us in these sketches some valuable and interesting reminiscences. The reading of a volume of *Lyrical Ballads*, written by Wordsworth and Coleridge, and published in 1799, was to him, he says, one of the greatest epochs of his life. "I found in these poems the ray of a new morning, and an absolute revelation of untrodden worlds teeming with power and beauty, as yet unsuspected among men." This was when the superfine critics of the day were exhausting epithets of abuse upon these two poets, when the name of the Lake School was a by-word of scorn, and the scoff of the literary world.

De Quincey and Professor Wilson were the first to stand in the breach of popular prejudice, and proclaim to the world that a true poet had arisen, even William Wordsworth. In this they anticipated the public taste, for who would attempt to laugh down Wordsworth now?

De Quincey's reminiscences of Wordsworth and Coleridge are, perhaps, the most valuable authentic records left of the life and character of these two men. His criticisms of their works are full of beauty and wise discrimination. They show us the true vocation of the poet, as an interpreter of the beautiful and true in all things, and of the higher feelings and instincts of humanity. The true poet is the representative of fact; nature speaks to him and through him. He loves nature for her rich dowry of truth and beauty, these he marries to his verse.

De Quincey's personal sketches of Wordsworth and Coleridge give us faithful portraits of these two great men, as they lived, loved, suffered, and acted. Wordsworth possessed not a warm, genial heart for friendship with his fellow men. "His soul was like a star that dwelt apart"; it loved abstractions and to commune with unseen things, rather than with their warm concrete union with flesh and blood. With Coleridge, De Quincey had more sympathy; and beautiful, yet sad, is the portrait drawn of him—"The rapt one with the godlike forehead." They could well sympathise with each other, for both had trodden the same path, "following the track of German metaphysicians, Latin schoolmen, theumaturgic Platonists, and religious mystics." Both had been the victims of the same inveterate habit which had prostrated their energies and produced an infirmity of will and purpose. He could feel a generous sympathy with that old man, settled in gloom, as he looked back upon a life wasted by bodily pains and infirmities, when the bright aspirations of youth lay like withered flowers at his feet. We are inclined to agree with Carlyle against De Quincey respecting this "old man eloquent," and cannot help thinking that much of Coleridge's talk was what it has been called, "transcendental moonshine." "Excellent talker, very," said Hazlitt, "if you let him start from no premises and come to no conclusion." In reading some of these wonderful displays of philosophical rigmarole, one is reminded of the old Scotchman's definition of metaphysics. "You see," says he, "twa folk disputen thegither; he that's listenin' does na ken what he that's speaken means; and he that's speaken does na ken what he means himsel'; that's metaphysics." "I have heard Coleridge talk," says Carlyle, "with eager, musical energy, two stricken hours, his face radiant and moist, and communicate no meaning whatsoever to any individual of his hearers." In these sketches of Coleridge and Wordsworth there is a fretful, egotistical spirit which here and there breaks out, casting reproachful aspersions upon their characters in private life. For instance, his remarks upon Coleridge's wife, and an account of some petty quarrels between himself and Wordsworth, exceed the proper bounds of biographical gossip.

There should be a spirit of reserve in speaking of a man's social and domestic life, especially in looking at those faults which are inseparable from our human nature. It is an old saying, of which we are proud, "that an Englishman's house is his castle"; it might also be added that his hearth is his temple, for around it are clustered the sanctities of life, and these should be held sacred from the intrusion and vulgar gaze of strangers.

In De Quincey's *Autobiographic Sketches* it is difficult to separate the imaginary from the real. Although he was perpetually writing about himself, yet it is extraordinary how very little he has revealed. From what we can gather of the later part of his life, it was a sorrowful one; neglected, broken down in health, compelled to fight against starvation with his pen, to fritter away his noble genius upon magazine articles, and to skip lightly over subjects which were of little interest beyond the passing moment; writing generally under great pressure as to time, in order to catch the critical period of monthly journals; oftentimes at a distance from the press and from libraries, so as to have no opportunities for correction; depending upon an unassisted memory for statements, references, &c.; suffering also under the distraction of a nervous misery, which embarrassed his efforts in a mode and in a degree wholly inexpressible by words. Under these circumstances the wonder is not only that he wrote so much, but wrote so well. This distressing nervous malady no doubt prevented him from applying himself to any great work worthy of his genius. As we go through his life, with its struggles and sorrows, we cannot but regard it as a commentary upon the lines of Goethe: "Where thou beholdest genius, there thou beholdest too the martyr's crown." How sad were his retrospections of life may be gathered from his own words: "Heavens! when I look back to the sufferings which I have witnessed or heard of, I say if life could throw open its long suites of chambers to our eyes from some station *beforehand*—if from some secret stand we could look by *anticipation* along its vast corridors, and aside into the recesses opening upon them from either hand, halls of tragedy, or chambers of retribution, simply in that small wing and no more of the great caravanserai which we ourselves shall haunt—simply in that narrow tract of time, and no more, where we ourselves shall range, and confining our gaze to those and no others for whom personally we shall be interested,—What a recoil we should suffer of horror in our estimate of life!" And again he says: "Death we can face; but knowing, as some of us do, what is human life, which of us is it that without shuddering could (if consciously were we summoned) face the hour of birth?"

In giving extracts from De Quincey's writings, we find a difficulty in making a selection; we will make one from an article on *The System of the Heavens as Revealed by Lord Ross's Telescope*, being a review of Professor Nichol's *Architecture of the Heavens*. This article gives a fair display of his literary powers; of his sly, insinuating, yet playful humour, and of his wonderful command of language. Here are found those sudden changes from the sublime to the ridiculous, and written in corresponding style. We shall quote an extract concluding the article, in which he has extended an idea to be found in Richter; it is entitled *Dream Vision of the Infinite as it Reveals itself in the Chambers of Space*:—

"God called up from dreams a man into the vestibule of Heaven, saying, 'Come up hither, and see the glory of my house.' And to the servants that stood around his throne, he said, 'Take him, and undress him from his robes of flesh; cleanse his vision, and put a new breath into his nostrils; only touch not with any change his human heart—the heart that weeps and trembles.' It was done; and with a mighty angel for his guide, the man stood ready for his infinite voyage; and from the terraces of heaven, without sound or farewell, at once they wheeled away into endless space. Sometimes, with the solemn flight of angel-wing, they fled through deserts of darkness—through wildernesses of death, that divided the worlds of life; sometimes they swept over frontiers, that were quickening under prophetic motions from God. Then from a distance that is counted only in heaven, light dawned for a time through a sleeply film; by unutterable pace the light swept to them, they by unutterable pace to the light. In a moment the rushing of planets was upon them; in a moment the blazing of suns was around them. Then came eternities of twilight, that revealed, but were not revealed. On the right hand and on the left towered mighty constellations, that by self-repetitions and answers from afar, that by counter-positions, built up triumphal gates, whose architraves, whose archways—horizontal, upright—rested, rose, at altitudes by spans—that seemed ghostly from infinitude. Without measure were the architraves, past number were the archways, beyond memory the gates. Within were stairs that scaled the eternities below! Above was below, below was above, to the man stripped of gravitating body; depth was swallowed up in height insurmountable, height was swallowed up in depth unfathomable. Suddenly, as thus they rode from infinite to infinite, suddenly, as thus they tilted over abysmal worlds, a mighty cry arose—that systems more mysterious, that worlds more billowy—other heights and other depths—were coming, were nearing, were at hand! Then the man sighed, and stopped, shuddered, and wept. His overladened heart uttered itself in tears, and he said, 'Angel, I will go no further; for the spirit of man acheth with this infinity. Insufferable is the glory of God's house. Let me lie down in the grave, and hide me from the persecution of the infinite; for end I see there is none.' And from all the listening stars that shone around issued a choral voice, 'The man speaks truly: end there is none, that ever yet we heard of.' 'End, is there none?' the Angel solemnly demanded: 'and is this the sorrow that kills you?' But no voice answered, that he might answer himself. Then the Angel threw up his glorious hands to the heaven of heavens, saying, "End is there none to the universe of God. Lo! also there is no beginning.'"

There is one article in his miscellanies we ought not to pass over, upon *Jean D'Arc*, which is full of manly earnestness, tender sympathy, and deep pathos. Well has he told her tale. He tells us how, when a *man* was not to be found in the crisis of a nation's history, a *woman* came forward, clad herself in armour, stood in the breach of danger, mingled in the shock of armies, and even gave her body to be burned, that from its ashes might spring up the seeds of liberty. Such a heroine was Jean D'Arc. We behold her as she comes forth from beneath the shadows of her native mountains, where silently her soul laboured in travail for the sorrows of her people, and where she had nursed those great thoughts under the inspiration of which sprung up armed men, who knew how to fight and to die—thoughts which gave her soul that unconquerable energy and will, which death itself could not intimidate, to proclaim her mission and to execute it. We see her cleaving her way through her enemy's legions, penetrating their strongholds, and leading on the Dauphin to be crowned at Rheims. We see her again in the toilet of Death, preparing for immortality.

Let anyone read this article without tears if they can. Such tears will do the heart good; they are not the simperings of sentimentality as evaporate over the pages of the last new novel, or "such tears as tender lawyers shed," for they evoke the highest sympathies of our nature, springing as they do from the deep fountain of the heart.

Yet there is one thing objectionable in this article, viz., a wild display of humour, dancing like sunbeams upon the bosom of some dark waters—the scene of an awful tragedy—or like a troop of merry children, gaily frolicking in the house of mourning and tears. There is evidently a struggle in the mind of the author to repress it, sometimes even by tears; but now and then it breaks out. We see it dancing even beneath the scaffold and upon the funeral pyre; yet it is not like the hollow laughter of those fiends who stood around their victim, exulting in their barbarity and revelling in their cruelty as they beheld her clad in fire. He does not laugh at her, but at her tormentors, who could do no more—who could not touch her beauteous spirit as it winged its way to another tribunal, there to stand in judgment against her false witnesses and executioners.

Thus have we endeavoured to give a rapid sketch of De Quincey's mind and writings. We feel that we have not done justice to his great powers in these faint jottings of ours; yet this man's life was imperfect, and his works are fragmentary; the deadly effects of opium paralysed his efforts for writing any monumental work; what he has done is not commensurate to what he might have done. He has not been a great teacher, one of the pioneers of his age, clearing barriers, and removing mountains to prepare the way for the grand march of humanity. But he has been more an interpreter than a teacher; more an instructor and pleasing companion than a guide. He has nestled into the brains of our greatest thinkers, and interpreted to us their thoughts; having been more a labourer at the mint than the mine, working up the sterling metal into current use. "His translations have enabled us to shake hands with brethren whom we knew not; the living, who to us were dead; and the dead who cannot die." Those who wish to become acquainted with the ancient and modern philosophies, whether of the Egyptian, Grecian, Latin, or German schools, let them peruse carefully the writings of Thomas De Quincey; for, as a subtle thinker, a clear reasoner, with a richly stored and well cultivated mind, with an eye to see, a heart to feel, and moreover, a strong poetic sympathy to enlighten and render these truths manifest, he is, we think, second to none of our modern writers.

MODERN CIVILIZATION:

Its Effects on Human Life, etc.

"The number of a man's days are at most one hundred years."
Ecclesiasticus xviii. 9.

Modern Civilization,
etc.

MAN lives in a world of wonders, and of all its marvels he is to himself the greatest. Although he is the only being who can contemplate his own existence, yet it may with truth be said, that nowhere is he so much a stranger as at home. As he looks within at his mysterious being, the question arises, What am I?—a rather puzzling one in the contentiousness of rival schools of philosophy. For there is the Materialist who denies him a soul, and the Idealist who denies him a body, and, then again, there are those who dispute the existence of both, who make matter a figment and mind also, who regard them as but names for the imaginary substrata of groups of natural phenomena. No wonder that as the novice puzzles his brain, which is not "large enough to lodge all these controversial intricacies," he should feel, like the student in *Faust*, "as if within his head a wheel was whirling round with ceaseless reel." According to his so-called "stupid common sense,"[*] he sees, or thinks he

---
[*] G. H. Lewes.

sees; he feels, or thinks he feels; at any rate, to him "pain is a reality;" and he often contents himself, at last, after the manner of the monkey, who, having dabbled in metaphysics satisfactorily to himself, solved the difficulty of the objective and the subjective by boiling his own tail, and was able at one and the same moment, not only to perceive objectively the process of boiling, but to be subjectively conscious of it. Again, as he looks abroad in the world, there are a number of questions which this sphinx-like age of inquiry is ever ready to propound to him, and which he must answer somehow at his peril. What is his place here? Was the earth made for him, or he for the earth? Is earth to earth his final resting-place, and that which is called the soul to pass away like an exhalation of gas or vapour, as the bodily compounds are reduced to their elements, in much the same way as the Buddhist believes in the final absorption of the spirit in Nervana; only the one is a material, and the other a spiritual dissolution? These are questions which knock at the door of his heart for answer; and if in his perplexity he seeks aid from science or philosophy, he finds that they only create more difficulties in his mind than they can solve, for "the greater the knowledge the greater the doubt."* Thus it befalls him who is taught to submit faith to reason instead of reason to faith, until he is often brought to the same conclusion as Voltaire's ignorant philosopher, who, after plunging himself with Thales into water as the first principle of all things, after roasting himself at the fire of Empedocles, after running in a straight line in the vacuum with Epicurus's atoms,

---

* Goethe.

after calculating numbers with Pythagoras and hearing his music, after paying his devoir to the Androgines of Plato, and passing through all the regions of metaphysics and of madness, "his wide voyaging" has found no home for his soul, and he is at last led to believe nothing because he can know nothing. It seems that man was not born to solve the great problems of his life and destiny. Shakespeare and Goethe, Bacon and Mill, Carlyle and Herbert Spencer, Tyndall and Huxley, can give us no more light than did Job or Solomon, Plato or Lucretius, &c. And alas, how many have found from bitter experience that the tree of knowledge is not the tree of life! and learned the truth of the sad text, "He that increaseth knowledge increaseth sorrow."

Because some of our philosophers cannot interpret the mystery of human existence, or penetrate into the arcana of nature, they have asserted, with an air of dignified conclusiveness, that nature is a great bungler, that she is irrational and immoral. We read of her clumsy provision for the perpetual renewal of animal life; how she tortures her victims, such as only the greatest monsters whom we read of ever purposely inflicted on their living fellow-creatures; that anarchy and the reign of terror are overmatched in injustice, ruin, and death, by a hurricane and a pestilence.* As we read these grave charges, we are reminded of Alphonse of Castile, who said that the universe was defective, and that, if he had been consulted in the making of it, he could have given many useful hints towards its improvement.

Putting aside the speculations and technicalities of

---

* J. S. Mill's *Essay on Nature.*

philosophy, we shall endeavour to take man as we find him, and to consider him in his relation to the world and to modern civilization.

In human life we reach nature's masterpiece. If there are mysteries in the lowest forms of organic life, and a blade of grass can puzzle a philosopher, how much more in that wondrous microcosm we call man! In looking at our bodies, at the complex machinery, the wonderful adjustment and adaptation of nerve and muscle, and the various processes of nature, well may we exclaim with the poet—

> "Tis strange that a harp with a thousand strings
> Should keep in tune so long."

The wonder is, not that we should die, but that we live, for our life consists in "dying daily." The first breath is the beginning of death. That which is alive to-day will be dead to-morrow. Every individual, it is said, wears out as many suits of bodies as he does of clothes; yet he remains the same living agent. "We have all been upon our trenchers," says Brown; "in brief, we have devoured ourselves," for we are self-fed and self-consumed. Life means destruction of tissue, and we exhaust energy by action; action of muscle produces destruction of muscle, action of mind destruction of mind; and that which is destroyed must be replaced by food and sleep, which periodically makes good the loss.

To solve the mystery of life has long been one of the endeavours of science. Granting all our modern discoveries, they have but pushed the difficulty a little further backward. According to the doctrine known as the Correlation of Forces, light, heat and electricity are not three things but one, variously set forth and mutually convertible. So vital force, says Dr. Carpenter, is correlated with light, heat, electricity, chemical affinity, or mechanical motion; and he declares that vital, mental, and nervous action are also modifications of the same force. But assuming this, there is still the mystery of force, whether we call it vital force or spiritual essence, or regard life as the sum total of all vital organism. We can only give names to that which is unknown. But if science cannot solve for us the mystery of life, it can teach us some of the laws by which our existence is sustained. Our civilization tends to elevate and extend human life, for its average duration was never higher than at present.*

The theory of Rousseau, of man's living the life of a savage as the natural state, is an untenable one, as savages are not long livers. Le Père Fauque, who lived much among them, says that he scarcely saw an old man; Raynal, Dr. Livingstone and others give the same testimony

---

* This is well shown in some statistics lately published by the authority of the Registrar General. Taking London, for example, the last three years show a marked reduction in the mortality, and imply an improvement of the health of the drained city. The annual mortality for the ten years 1840-49, was 35·2; for the 35 years 1840-74, it was 24·2; for the last three years, 1872-74, it was 22-2. Upon the population of 1874, the reduction in the mortality of three in one thousand implies a diminution of 10,200 deaths a year, equal to the population of a moderate-sized town. But there still remains much to be done, especially in decreasing the mortality of children among the poorer classes. Taking an area of the West End of London, and comparing it with an equal area occupied by the working classes, it has been ascertained that the richer district, with one-sixth of the population, rears twice as many children as the poorer.

from different parts of the world. The tendency of civilization is to promote physical grace and symmetry of form as well as health. Savages and half barbaric men and women are not remarkable for their beauty, but rather otherwise, if the poet sings truly—

> "Of Lapland's filthy people,
> Flat-headed, wide-mouthed, we spake;
> How they sit round their fires and jabber,
> And shriek o'er the fish they bake."

The highest moral and mental culture a man can attain is that which is most compatible with his nature. "Is not that the best education which gives to the mind and the body all the force. all the beauty, and all the perfection of which they are capable?"* It is this cultivation which renders man useful even to extreme age. Among savages old men are of no account, as they can no longer hunt or fight; and for this reason, with some of the most degraded races, a limit is put upon the length of human life, and the aged and helpless are killed. This horrid custom seems to have existed from time immemorial, as Herodotus mentions some of the barbaric nations fixing the duration of human life by law. But in civilized countries the aged are respected, and their experience and ripe judgment made available where the people are governed by the wisest, who are mostly men of mature age.

In the present busy, active, struggling life in our densely populated cities, incessant toil and worry kill men through the brain. It seems in these days that we have quite forgotten St. Paul's admonition, "Study to be quiet."

---

* Plato.

This restless activity and high pressure of our lives is, perhaps, one of the curses of our existing state of civilization.

> "Life treads on life, and heart on heart,
> We press too close in Church and mart,
> To keep a dream or grave apart."

We kill ourselves to save time in order often to merely kill time. "We have," says the cynic, "the railroad that hurries about persons who have nothing to do, and the telegraph that conveys the words of people who have nothing to say." The evil effects of life in our large towns show themselves in the statistics of town and country mortality, in England, the mean annual mortality in the large towns being about 23 or 24 in 1000, while that of the whole kingdom does not exceed 20 in the same number. No doubt it is not time that kills so much as worry; for time does his work honestly and well. "With our customs, our passions, our miseries, man does not die," says Flourens, "he kills himself." Apart from the weary struggle for life of the bread-winner, and the particular occupations which tend to shorten existence, there is also the excessive tension at which the mental faculties are kept so many hours each day, for so many months of the year, in the vortex of city life, by the keen competition and never-ending struggle for social and professional position, which produces a wear and tear of body and mind, inducing premature decay. "A man," says Dr. Johnson, "is never more harmlessly employed than in the making of money." This is true if he does not bow down body and soul to worship it when he has made it. An ordinary Englishman's education, politics, and religion, all seem to turn on one subject—how to make money. In this respect we somewhat resemble the ancient Romans; and how often is the poet Horace's satirical maxim adopted—"Make a fortune, if you can honestly; if not, a fortune by any means!" though, unlike the luxurious Roman, it is not always in the present day that wealth is sought after for the sake of comfort, abundance, or physical enjoyment. To acquire riches needs self-sacrifice, and often rigorous self-denial, which are sometimes carried too far, until the whole enjoyment is in the pursuit, and not in the possession. A writer in *Fraser's Magazine,* some time ago, well described a life which is a familiar one to those who have had experience in our large towns. "Our poor friend Robinson has made one fortune, but did not consider it large enough, and is now busy making another. He is off to the city at eight a.m., never returning till eight p.m., and then so worn and jaded that he cares for nothing beyond his dinner and his sleep. His beautiful house, his conservatories and pleasure grounds, delight not him; he never enjoys, he only pays for them. He has a charming wife, and a youthful family, but he sees little of them; the latter, indeed, he never sees at all except on Sundays. He comes home so tired that the children would only worry him. To them 'papa' is almost a stranger. They know him only as a periodical encumbrance on the household life, which generally makes it much less pleasant. And when they grow up, it is to such a totally different existence that they quietly ignore him. 'Oh! papa cares nothing about this. No, no; we never think of telling papa anything.' Until some day papa will die, and leave them a quarter of a million. But how much better to leave them what no money can ever buy—the remembrance of a *father!* A real father, whose guardianship made home safe; whose tenderness filled it with happiness; who was companion and friend, as well as ruler and guide; whose influence inter-penetrated every day of their lives—every feeling of their hearts; who was not merely 'the author of their being,' that is nothing, a mere accident, but the originator and educator of everything good in them; the visible father on earth, who made them understand dimly 'our Father which is in heaven.'"

If there is a gospel of labour, there is also a gospel of rest; and if the true philosophy of life is the right use of all things, the right use of time is one of the most important. But we must not confound rest with idleness. We never need be idle; weariness of body may often be relieved by mental occupation, and after mental exertion body and mind are refreshed by active physical exercise; but brain activity or bodily activity must not be pushed too far. The due exercise of the brain in thought is one of the essential elements of our existence. A maudlin, yawning, stupid life is not only a miserable, but it is an unhealthy one. We all know how by disuse a limb becomes weak and shrivelled, the muscles emaciated, and lose their power of action; and so far as regards exercise, the brain is no exception to the general rule, for it is under the same laws as the other organs of the body.

Variety of occupation is as essential for the health of the mind as of the body. The mind finds relief in a *change of study*. If the ideas are always running in one groove, on the same line of thought, the wear and tear is great, and a little shunting is necessary. Perhaps the reason why lawyers as a rule do not break down so often, and are longer lived than clergymen, is because their studies are not so exclusive, for diversified mental work does not produce the evil effects that monotonous labour does. J. S. Mill said that he found office duties an actual rest from the other severe mental occupations which he carried on simultaneously with them. So we find one of our great statesmen in his leisure moments writing novels, another translating Homer, &c.

The investigations of Professor Ferrier into the functions of the brain have established beyond a doubt that the brain is the organ of the mind, and that it is duplex. He has proved by direct excitation of the fibres of various parts of the brain, that "each part, if not each fibre, has a distinct mental function, and produces specific emotions and specific actions." Now, if men exercise only one part of the brain, it will be at the expense of the other. Thus we find that, in the savage, the cerebellum, or little brain, which undoubtedly has considerable share in muscular co-ordination, is larger than in the European. The existence of the savage is dependent upon agility and muscular activity, and the larger development of this portion of the brain is, no doubt, due to long training and exercise. In the European the cerebrum, or big brain, which is supposed to be pre-eminently, if not exclusively, devoted to the intellectual actions, is larger than in the savage. The European is more dependent upon mental activity, and this exercise we may suppose enlarges the amount of cerebrum and deepens its convolutions. But by disuse the brain becomes inactive, the cerebral tissue disorganized, and intellectual decay follows. "The human heart," says Luther, and we may apply the same remark to the human mind, "is like a millstone in a mill. When you put wheat under it, it turns, and grinds, and bruises the wheat into flour. If you put no wheat in, it still grinds on; but then it is itself it grinds, and slowly wears away." We believe that when brain-work is injurious it is so in consequence of faulty methods rather than of excess, when there is great mental exertion without any physical equilibrium. Some of the greatest thinkers have been among the longest livers. The leading public men of all countries, notwithstanding their severe mental labour and excitement of their anxious life, generally reach old age. In fact the brain-workers seem to outlive ordinary men. Kant, who lived to a great age, said that "intellectual pursuits tend to prolong life." The French Academy is, perhaps, the most learned body in the world, and the ages of the youngest members average from 60 to 70. Within the last few years five great lawyers—Eldon, Stowell, Lyndhurst, Brougham, and St. Leonards—have passed their ninetieth year. Great natural philosophers, poets, and painters, have generally been long livers. It has been humorously said that the diploma of a royal academician seems to be a grant of a longer lease of life, among its other advantages. Philosophers are proverbially long livers; this may arise from their calm steady habits of thought, and wise discipline of mind and body. Philosophy, it is said, will not bake our bread; but it may teach us how to live; and he is truly a philosopher who is indifferent to the smiles and frowns of fortune, who maintains the calm dignity of self-control through all the vicissitudes of life. In this sense our religion ought to be the highest philosophy. As an illustration of this habit of mind, which is quite as much a matter of discipline as of nature, we will quote a passage from Dean Stanley's funeral sermon upon Lord Palmerston. After speaking of the continued perseverance and unfailing hopefulness of the departed statesman, he says, "Nor let us shut out the encouragement which this is designed to give us, by saying, that it was for him only a natural result of a buoyant and vigorous constitution. To a great degree, no doubt, it was; yet it also rested in a large measure on the deeper ground of a quiet conviction that the fitting course for man was to do what was good for the moment, without forecasting the future—to do the present duty, and to leave the result with God." "I do not understand," he once said, to one who knew him well—"I do not understand what is meant by the anxiety of responsibility. I take every pains to do what is for the best, and having done that, I am perfectly at ease, and leave the consequences altogether alone."

But there arises the question, How many men really die from overtaxing the brain? In nearly every case a medical practitioner will trace brain-disease to an essentially physical cause which is referable to the disturbance of the normal action of the blood upon the brain. It is said that the excessive use of alcohol and tobacco produces far more softening of the brain and heart-disease among students than hard study. The want of exercise, also the lack of rest, hastily and ill-digested meals, and anxiety *about* their work, are enough to break down many students and hard-worked professional men, without any brain-work at all. It is only by the study of bodily habit that the physiology of mental habit can be properly understood: a healthy mind and a healthy body can only go together. The outside world receives its colouring from the mind, and the mind sees through the body. When we are bright within everything is bright without; and when the soul is under an eclipse it is "dark, dark, amid the blaze of noon." Hood has well depicted two opposite states of feeling which undoubtedly in his case were of physical origin:—

> "Farewell Life! my senses swim,
> And the world is growing dim;
> Thronging shadows cloud the light,
> Like the advent of the night,—
> Colder, colder, colder still,
> Upward steals a vapour chill,
> Strong the earthly odour grows,
> I smell the mould above the rose!"
>
> "Welcome Life! the spirit strives!
> Strength returns, and hope revives;
> Cloudy fears and shapes forlorn
> Fly like shadows at the morn,—
> O'er the earth there comes a bloom,
> Sunny light for sullen gloom.
> Warm perfume for vapours cold—
> I smell the rose above the mould!"

How many of the so-called miseries of existence arise from that functional derangement of the stomach which is commonly known as indigestion! A well-known American physician, Dr. Brigham, attributes indigestion to the brain instead of the stomach. "Dyspepsia," he says, "is generally considered a disease of the stomach primarily. But I apprehend that in a majority of cases, especially among students, it is primarily a disease of the brain and nervous system, and is perpetuated by mental excitement." In proof of this theory he shows that dyspepsia is not known in countries where people eat enormously. Travellers in Siberia say that the people there often eat forty pounds of food in one day, yet dyspepsia is unknown amongst them. The Esquimaux are not nervous and dyspeptic, though they individually eat ten or twelve pounds of solid food in a day, washing it down with a gallon or so of train oil. Captain Lyon mentions a delicate young lady Esquimaux, who ate his candles, wicks and all, yet he does not allude to her inability to digest them! De Quincey was disposed to think that the brain and the stomach apparatus, through their reciprocal action and reaction, jointly make up the compound organ of thought. But whether this disease arises primarily from the brain or the stomach, there can be no doubt that if digestion is impeded, from whatever cause, the mind suffers. "I tell you honestly what I think," says Abernethy, "is the cause of the complicated maladies of the human race—it is the gormandizing, and stuffing, and stimulating their organs (the digestive) to excess, thereby producing nervous disorders and irritations. *The state of their minds is another grand cause; the fidgeting and discontenting yourselves about what cannot be helped;* passions of all kinds—malignant passions pressing upon the mind, disturb the cerebral action, and do much harm." Sydney Smith has humorously described some of these miseries and their consequences. He says—" Happiness is not impossible without health, but it is of very difficult attainment. I do not mean by health merely an absence of dangerous complaints, but that the body should be in perfect tune, full of vigour and alacrity. The longer I live, the more I am convinced that the apothecary is of more importance than Seneca; and that half the unhappiness in the world proceeds from little stoppages, from a duct choked up, from food pressing in the wrong place, from a vexed duodenum, or an agitated pylorus. The deception, as practised upon human creatures, is curious and entertaining. My friend sups late: he eats some strong soup, then a lobster, then some tart, and he dilutes these esculent varieties with wine. The next day I call upon him. He is going to sell his house in London, and to retire into the country. He is alarmed for his eldest daughter's health. His expenses are hourly increasing, and nothing but a timely retreat can save him from ruin. All this is the lobster; and when over-excited nature has had time to manage this testaceous encumbrance, the daughter recovers, the finances are in good order, and every rural idea effectally excluded from the mind."

"In the same manner, old friendships are destroyed by toasted cheese, and hard salted meat has led to suicide. Unpleasant feelings of the body produce correspondent sensations in the mind, and a great scene of wretchedness is sketched out by a morsel of indigestible misguided food. Of such infinite consequence to happiness is it to study the body." As a pendant to these observations upon brainwork, we may observe that in the opinion of one of our greatest physiologists, "Mere intellectual activity, when unaccompanied by agitating emotion, never seems to affect digestion, unless the effort be of an unusual intensity. Our passions are destroying flames: Anger, Ambition, Envy, Despair, Sorrow, and even Sudden Joy immediately disturb the digestion."

One of the questions which has always been interesting in almost every age is that of the duration of human life, yet it is surrounded by so many difficulties, and has been such a matter of idle speculation and exaggeration, that it is only within the last few years the subject has been considered upon any rational or scientific basis. This life of ours which is given us only once to live, ought in truth to have some concern for us. Most of us desire to live long, but none of us wish for old age, and, strange anomaly, those who have wasted life seem the most anxious to extend it, as those who have the most leisure have the least time to do anything. A life is not misspent, if as we grow older we grow wiser; and a life sacrificed for truth and duty is better than one saved for the mere sake of existence. It is not functional vitality so much as activity of mind which truly constitutes our living—

> "We live in deeds, not years; in thoughts, not breaths;
> In feelings, not in figures on a dial.
> We should count time by heart-throbs. He most lives
> Who thinks most, feels the noblest, acts the best."

What a man is must be estimated by what he does, and his manhood by his capability for thought and affection. The soul must be measured by its desires: give a pig the wealth of El Dorado, yet his aspirations would never rise beyond his trough and garbage. But man cannot be made happy through his senses alone, and happiness does not come to him who seeks it, but to him who has an object beyond and independent of it.

Much has been written lately upon the longevity of man, and most of the recorded monstrosities of life's duration are shown to have been apocryphal,* and many so-called centenarians have been shorn of their hoary honours, when severe chronological tests have been applied. In the records of fabulous longevity, such as Henry Jenkins, attaining the age of 169, Old Parr, the age of 152, and the old Countess of Desmond, 140, &c., there is no register, certificate, or scrap of real evidence which would be of any use in a court of justice to support their claim; and we must remember that in most cases only the bare word of the supposed centenarians themselves.

In some assertions of extreme longevity there may be much self-deception, especially as regards the supposed early recollections. The writer for a long time believed that he recollected persons who died before he was born, and it was with great difficulty that he could disabuse his mind of the impossibility of his ever having remembered them. This is the experience of many. Portraits, people and events much talked about are impressed upon the mind of children at an early age, and the imagination afterwards puts them into a tangible shape. But there have been cases of great imposture, such as Fuller wittily and quaintly describes, where "many old men used to set the clock of their age too fast when past seventy, and growing ten years a twelvemonth are presently four-score; yea, within a year or two climb up to a hundred." Dates and inscriptions on tombstones must be very guardedly taken as evidence of abnormal longevity. Most of us have wandered into a quiet county churchyard, scanned o'er the

* See Mr. W. T. Thom's work on *Human Longevity; its Facts and Fictions.*

simple records of the dead, and smiled at the eccentric verses, but some of the dates are as curious as the epitaphs. Two or three cases quoted by Mr. Thom's, from the *Quarterly Review, Notes and Queries*, &c., are very amusing. "At Chave Priory, in Worcestershire, there is one which ascribes to an old forefather of the hamlet the goodly length of 309 years. But the record meant nothing patriarchal. The village chiseller, hazy about numeration, wished to score 39, and engraved 30 first and 9 afterwards. In the churchyard of Bickenhill, Warwickshire, is a tombstone to the memory a Mrs. Ann Smith, who died in 1701. It states that she died a maid, and deceased aged 708! At Stratford-on-Avon some workmen engaged in the restoration of the church about the year 1839, having found a gravestone in which there happened to be a space before the age 72, for the honour of the place, and it is expected with the consent of the sexton, inserted the figure 1 in the space, and so changed the year 72 into 172. In a parish church in Kent, a man whose fourth wife survived him, was described as having departed this life in the 11th year of his age."

Sir G. C. Lewis, after investigating the subject of longevity, came to the conclusion that no clear recorded case had been made out of man's attaining a century; but he modified his opinions before his death, as many such cases have been verified. Although insurance offices have been in existence since 1706, their books have furnished testimony to only one centenarian; but half-a-dozen cases have been well attested within the last few years. Mr. Brabrook, F.S.A., recently supplied Mr. Thom's with particulars from the National Debt Office of three cases of undoubted centenarian annuitants.* Many books have been written upon the art of prolonging life, but up to the present the subject has been mostly treated by the quack, whose principal qualification for the work is that he is profoundly ignorant of the matter, and that in his practise he uses the best means for shortening life, as we may be sure that he who professes to cure all diseases can cure none. The strict rules and regulations given for longevity are generally such that after a great deal of perseverance and careful attention to diet, exercise, &c., the patient, by making living the great business of his life, at last succeeds at about middle age in killing himself.

It is related of the celebrated Lord Montboddo, that when he was engaged in writing a treatise on longevity, he visited an old Scotch lady, reputed to be 101 years of age, and the following dialogue took place between them.

Lord M.—" I presume, Madam, you've been in the habit of frequent ablutions, and often bathe ?"

Old Lady.—" Na ! Na ! I'm no fond o' floutering in cold water."

Lord M.—" Then, Madam, you've anointed your body with oils ?"

Old Lady.—" Na ! Na ! Fie, ye nasty creetur."

Lord M.—" Then you've always taken exercise very regularly."

Old Lady.—" Ou ! I gang to the kirk on Sabbath, and whiles to the market; but I'm no fond o' walking."

Lord M.—" I presume you are rigidly temperate—even abstemious ?"

---

* See *Journal of the Anthropological Institute*, July, 1875.

Old Lady.—" Na! Na! I tak' my toddy at dinner, and a wee drappie at bed-time."

The noble lord, finding all his preconceived theories set at naught, rose and said :—

" Madam, had you done all I've given you credit for, you'd have been immortal."

In searching for cases of longevity one meets with a similar experience as the noble lord's. The "monstrosities of life duration," like all other monstrosities, are inexplicable. We cannot tell why a man should live 100 years any more than one should grow to eight feet, or another weigh 20 stone. It is very difficult to tell what is the average specific longevity of man, for the duration of life is much longer in one nation than another. The European reaches the highest average—about 40 years. This average is greatly lowered in consequence of the deaths in infancy. In London, for instance, out of 100 children born rather more than 72 attain the age of three years.* In Berlin, according to reliable statistics, one out of every three children born die the first year. The Anglo-Saxon race seems to possess, through some congenital organization and dynamic speciality, an exceptional vigour and power of vital resistance which gives it a greater potential longevity, or longer lease of life, than any other race on the globe. The Fuegians and other degraded races are stated rarely to exceed 45. At that age they are generally killed and eaten by their children, in order that they may escape,

---

* The difference between town and country mortality among children is something appalling. In country districts the number of children who die under five years is about 39 per 1,000, while the number in towns is 103 per 1,000.

what they consider, the dishonour of entering the world of spirits in a state of decrepitude.* It is a curious fact that some of the native Australian tribes have no idea of death arising from natural causes. When a man dies from disease or accident he is thought to have been murdered, and every means are taken to discover and punish the supposed murderer.

The population of the world—which is not supposed to be yet a quarter peopled—has been estimated at about 1,000,000,000 of persons, speaking 3,064 languages, and professing 1,100 forms of religion. The average duration of life is estimated at 33 years and 6 months; one quarter of mankind dying before their 7th year, and one-half before their 17th. Most nations speak of the age of man as being from 60 to 100, which indicate the same opinion with respect to the duration of life and excessive longevity. The ancient Egyptians, according to one of their monumental inscriptions, estimated the extreme duration of human life at 110 years. M. Flourens fixes 100 years as the normal life of man, on the principle that there is an exact ratio between the period occupied in growing to maturity and the full term or lease of existence, the same physiological law prevailing through the whole of the mammalia. Aristotle, who seems to have studied everything, put forth a similar

---

* Herodotus mentions a similar custom among the Massagetes, who, after a man had attained old age, his relatives met and sacrificed him, with cattle of several kinds, and, when they had boiled all the flesh together, they sat down as to a feast. This death they accounted the most happy, for they never ate the bodies of those who died by sickness, but buried them in the earth. And it was counted a great misfortune not to be sacrificed.

doctrine; and Buffon, who went into the subject carefully, taught that every animal lives, or at least is competent to live, from six to seven times as many years as it consumes in growing; and he lays it down that, in absence of sickness or accident, man actually ought to live 90 or 100 years.

"One thing," says M. Flourens, "was unknown to Buffon, viz., the sign that marks the term of growth. Now growth continues in all animals until the bones are united to the epiphyses. The epiphyses is a portion of bone, separated from the body of the bone by cartilage, which becomes converted into bone by age. When once the bones and their epiphyses are united, the animal grows no more. The real relation of the period of growth to the duration of life is as one to five, or nearly so. Man is 20 years growing, and he lives five times 20 years, or to 100; the camel is 8 years growing, and he lives to 40; the horse is 5 years growing, and he lives to 25; and so on to other animals. We have then at last an accurate criterion which gives us with certainty the period of growth: the duration of that period gives us the duration of life."

But M. Flouren's theory, like many other theories, explains too much; yet it does not truly represent all the facts, nor does it include all the laws to which observation and induction lead. Lord Holland says, " We doubt much whether this period of epiphyses, or completion of bony union, has been determined in a sufficient number of animals, and with sufficient exactness to serve as a basis for numerical results."

In order approximately to estimate the determined length of life in man, we must put aside imaginary data, or vague notions, based upon pre-conceived ideas, and enter into another important branch of inquiry, which has become in our days a new instrument of scientific research, viz., statistics; and opened up to us a wide field of inferential conclusions, drawn from facts extracted from the returns of the Registrar-General, and tables of life assurance. Nowhere, and at no time, have 100 years been the normal life of man. The argument that man ought to live a century, barring disease or accident, is much the same as saying that if there were no causes of death, man would not die. "What an idle conceit it is," says Montaigne, "to expect to die of a decay of strength, which is the last of effects of the extremest age, and to propose to ourselves no shorter lease of life than that, considering it is a kind of death of all others the most rare, and very hardly seen! We call that only a natural death, as if it were contrary to nature to see a man break his neck with a fall, be drowned in shipwreck at sea, or snatched away with a pleurisy, or the plague, and, as if our ordinary condition of life did not expose us to these inconveniences. To die of old age is a death rare, extraordinary, and singular; and, therefore, less natural than the others." The conclusions of Flourens find no place in the experience of mankind, nor in the general law of averages.

Again, though there may be signs to mark growth in man and the lower animals, yet, unlike the latter, there are in him no sure signs to mark age. For instance, the age of fishes appears to be marked on their scales, and that of the molluscous animals in the strata of their shells, in birds from the wear and form of their bills, the horse from its teeth, and the deer from its horns, and so on. But with man the case is different; some seem to reach old age sooner than others. Instances have been known where children have ceased to grow, and to exhibit signs of senile deterioration at 11 years. So much depends on constitution and temperament. Some lives burn quicker and more intense than others; they are consumed internally by their own fire. With others the lamp of life burns slowly; they are of a cold phlegmatic temperament, with, says the poet, "Souls that can scarce ferment their mass of clay." How often we see upon a young face an appearance of premature decay, "like a worm in the bud"! In others, again, we see a bronze-like countenance with a hardness of texture, and an outward appearance of iron strength, and rigour of soul which time can hardly impress and death can hardly conquer. Thus we find that some are born with a greater potential longevity than others, and we think that it will be impossible for science ever to fix a criterion for the specific longevity of man.

After all, we cannot go beyond the sublime words of the Psalmist, "The days of our years are three-score years and ten, and if by reason of strength they be fourscore years, yet is their strength labour and sorrow, for it is soon cut off, and we flee away." "By appointed laws," says Goethe, "we enter into life; the days are numbered which make us ripe to see the light; but for the duration of our life there is no law. The weakest thread will spin itself to unexpected length, and the strongest is cut suddenly asunder by the scissors of the fates, delighting as it seems in contradictions." Let us, then, live to a moderate age, and be thankful, for much may be accomplished within the allotted time of man. Some lives are more complete at 30 than others at 60. Many of the greatest names in History, Poetry and Art fulfilled their mission and finished their work when young. We might mention Alexander, Raphael, Mozart, Schiller, Burns, Keats, Byron, and a host of others. One of the great secrets of success is to know what to do, and how to do it, so as not to waste time in vain endeavours. Our life is too short to do many things *well*. "I once on a time," said Dr. Johnson, "took to fiddling; but I found that to fiddle well I must fiddle all my life, and I thought I could do something better." Porson, with his gigantic exhaustive brain said "Life was too short to learn German," that is, as he would have learnt it.

It is a sad thought to most of us how small a portion of our time we have left for our mental and moral improvement. Our lives are nearly all absorbed in the pursuit of merely temporal objects. Take three-score years and ten, and analyse them: a sum total of 25,550 days. Out of this total, "sleep, the brother of death," extracteth one-third of our lives; then deducting a large portion of our earlier life before the judgment is matured; another one-third must be extracted from most men for professional and business avocations; after making other deductions for illness, eating, and drinking, &c., how small a residue have we left before "The night cometh when no man can work"! The hand of mercy weaveth the veil of the future. We know not our portion for the morrow, which is a day of darkness; but it is something to know that He who conceals is He who directs and assists. We have all taken of the elixir of life, and our portion is immortality; for we shall live always, but not here. What is that awful unknown "self" or "soul"? Is it a matter of cells and fibres, of fat and phosphorus, of many and deep cerebral convolutions, a chemical laboratory for secreting thoughts? No! The soul, secure in its existence, defies the materialist, and by its intuition laughs to scorn his induction. "I am!" is its own proof, and no syllogism can touch it.

"Where, in the plan of Nature," says the German writer, Reimar, "do we find instincts falsified? Where do we see an instance of a creature instinctively craving a certain kind of food, in a place where no such food can be found? Are the swallows deceived by their instinct when they fly away from clouds and storms to seek a warmer country? Do they not find a milder climate beyond the water? When the May-flies and other aquatic insects leave their shells, expand their wings, and soar from the water into the air, do they not find an atmosphere filled to sustain them in a new stage of life? Yes. The voice of Nature does not utter false prophecies. It is the call, the invitation, of the Creator addressed to His creatures. And if this be true with regard to the impulses of physical life, why should it not be true with regard to the superior instincts of the soul?"

TABLE

Showing the Age attained by some of the most notable Literary Persons in Ancient and Modern Times.

Name.	Age.	Country.	Name.	Age.	Country.
Æschylus	69	Greece	Crabbe	73	England
Angelo	90	Italy	Cuvier	63	Germany
Anacreon	85	Anatolia	Coleridge	62	England
Archimedes	75	Greece	Copernicus	70	Poland
Aristotle	63	Greece			
Ariosto	59	Italy	Dante	56	Italy
			De Foe	71	England
Bacon, Lord	65	England	De Quincey	75	England
Bacon, Roger	78	England	Demosthenes	59	Greece
Bayle	59	France	Descartes	54	France
Bentham	84	England	Diderot	71	France
Berkeley	69	England	Dickens	58	England
Boccaccio	61	Italy	Dryden	70	England
Brougham	90	Scotland			
Buffon	81	France	Erasmus	69	Holland
Butler, Joseph	60	England	Euripides	75	Greece
Burke	67	Ireland	Euler	76	Switzerland
Burns	37	Scotland			
Byron	36	England	Fénélon	63	France
Bunyan	60	England			
			Galileo	78	Italy
Camoens	55	Portugal	Gall	70	Germany
Camden	73	England	Galen	79	Anatolia
Campbell, Thos.	67	Scotland	Gibbon	57	England
Cervantes	69	Spain	Goethe	83	Germany
Chaucer	71	England	Gray	55	England
Condillac	65	France			
Confucius	73	China	Hamilton, Sir W.	68	Scotland
Corneille	78	France	Halley	86	England
Congreave	57	England	Herschel	84	Germany

Name.	Age.	Country.	Name.	Age.	Country.
Hippocrates	109	Isle of Cos	Ovid	57	Italy
Hobbes	91	England			
Homer	60	Greece	Paley	62	England
Horace	57	Italy	Petrarch	70	Italy
Huber	82	Geneva	Pestalozzi	82	Switzerland
Hume	65	Scotland	Plato	82	Greece
Hutton, W.	92	England	Pope	56	England
			Pindar	80	Greece
Jenner	74	England	Rabelais	70	France
Johnson, Dr.	74	England	Racine	60	France
			Richter	62	Germany
Kant	80	Germany	Rousseau	66	Switzerland
Keats	26	England			
			Seneca	71	Spain
Lamb	59	England	Schiller	46	Germany
Landor	89	England	Scott, Sir W.	62	Scotland
Laplace	78	France	Shakespeare	52	England
Leibnitz	70	Germany	Simonides	89	Greece
Linnæus	71	Sweden	Smith, Adam	67	Scotland
Locke	73	England	Southey	69	England
Luther	63	Germany	Sophocles	90	Greece
			Swedenborg	85	Sweden
Malebranche	78	France	Swift	78	Ireland
Massillon	79	France			
Marmontel	79	France	Tacitus	76	Italy
Milton	66	England			
Mill, James	63	Scotland	Virgil	51	Italy
Mill, J. S.	67	England	Voltaire	84	France
Mirabeau	86	France			
Molière	53	France	Wordsworth	80	England
Montaigne	60	France	Young	80	England
Newton	85	England	Zeno	98	Cyprus

HEROISM:
A Lecture.

WE all love to hear of great men and of their heroic deeds. The child has his Pantheon, in which perhaps Jack the Giant Killer is the principal figure. It may not be generally known that Jack, like many other names of nursery tradition, is a hero of great antiquity, for it is said that he landed in England from the very same keels and war ships which conveyed Hengist, and Horsa, and Ebba the Saxon. Nearly all our nursery tales are remnants of heathen mythology. That fierce, cannibal giant, whose terrible fee-faw-fum reverberates even now in the dream-echoes of our childhood, belongs also to the mythology of our Danish ancestors, who derived it and others from the Aryan race in India. Our earliest traditions made men descended from gods in contradiction to our latest scientific speculations, which make them the children of monkeys. In the ancient Oriental fables, as well as those of Greece, Rome, and the Middle Ages, the hero was a demi-god, and a halo of poetic glory was thrown around him. The epics of Homer, the Scandinavian Scald, the poems of Ossian, and the Chronicle of the Cid, &c., were but the nucleus of floating traditions which the poet and the minstrel preserved. We may trace one truth, running like a golden thread through all these traditions, viz., that the world is governed by men of thought and men of action. Force of mind, of character, ever has and ever will rule the world, however we may try by wise laws and institutions to make our system of government self-supporting. At all times there have been, and we believe there will ever be, men, who by the combination of strong will with high moral resolve, are ready, for the sake of conscience and duty, to dare, to do, and to die. It is some consolation to know that when a man is wanted he appears, and that the selection is not of earth, but of heaven; it would be a denial of providence to assert otherwise.

But the world does not always know its greatest and wisest men. The prophet, as of old, is not often honoured in his time and country.

"Amidst his own
A stranger oft, companionless and lone,
God's priest and prophet stands."

The king clothed in purple has sometimes been but a puppet, the plaything of an hour, passing away with it, and becoming as a beggar in the eye of fame; while, on the other hand, the beggar who lived before his hour has written for all time his Iliad, and the world has clothed him in the immortal robes of honour and renown.

"Ten ancient towns contend for Homer dead,
Through which the living Homer begged his bread."

One of the chief causes why our greatest teachers are not always recognised in their age is, that the present is generally regarded as commonplace, for men are prone to worship the past. The historian and novelist weave their magic web of poetic prose and romance out of the past, and though a great man requires a certain focal distance to be seen, yet after all it is the ideal, and not the real man presented to our view. Your darling hero was to common eyes a common man, who ate, drank, lived and loved, had his little passions and failings, and if men could not take his measure, or if he lived in a spirit of antagonism to his age, he was called—well, people shake their heads and point the finger to the forehead, and mysteriously hint that he was a little touched there.

It is often such who have to endure deep wrongs from men, and scorn and chains, and sometimes to wear the martyr's crown; and every noble crown, says Carlyle, " is and on earth ever will be a crown of thorns," and many men have lived unknown " Till persecution dragged them into fame and chased them up to heaven."

Perhaps such an environment is necessary for the full development of genius and for progress in the world. If God tempers the wind to the shorn lamb, he forms the oak, which will not flourish in a hot bed, to grow stronger, to shoot upwards and downwards, as it withstands the might and fury of the tempest. But there has arisen lately a new race of egotists amongst us, who in their conceit of the present despise the past, who regard history as but an old almanac, and the wisdom and learning of our forefa·hers as folly. It is their fashion to despise metaphysics and extol the physical sciences, as if the study of the material universe of wood, iron and coal, of beasts, birds, and fishes was more profitable than that of God's noblest work—Man. Did not the Great Teacher invite us to

"Consider the lilies of the field and to behold the fowls of the air," that he might impress upon us the lesson, "Are ye not much better than they?"

Attempts have been made of late to make scepticism popular; but scepticism, except to a few minds, is always painful. True philosophy seeks rather to solve than to deny. It is only the fool, who, by believing as little as he can, thinks himself wise. He is a bigot, whose incurable narrow mind has been well compared to the pupil of the eye; the more light you let into it, the more it contracts; and in these days there is a vast and comprehensive ignorance which passeth for profound knowledge, which, under the guise of materialism and atheism, send forth from the drowsy twilight of their dismal caves the unsubstantial spectres of fear, mistrust, and despair, and all the brood of that "mis-shaped, miserable monster, Doubt," so that many men quake and cower down for fear of the heavens falling. Yet, on the other hand, there is a gross rage for comfortable sensualism and a warm materialism, the result of our continued prosperity, which is enervating. And it behoves us to keep the memory of the great and the heroic before us, that we may study human nature in its highest and noblest attributes, so as to be brought into contact with some of those who, by their brave acts and noble thoughts, make us feel that what they were we ought to strive to be.

Though we shall give some shining examples of great men, yet we must not forget that every one who is living a true life, and endeavouring to develop the best and noblest part of his nature, is a hero. According to Socrates, "the best man is he who tries to perfect himself and the happiest man is he who most feels that he is perfecting himself." We need not wait to do some grand thing, but live honestly and uprightly our every-day lives; we shall find all our strength needful to do that.

> " Who does the best his circumstance allows,
> Does well, acts nobly ; angels could no more."

One of the greatest monsters we have to fight against is Fear. "There is nothing," says Montaigne, "I fear so much as fear." The only way to conquer this weakness, is always to do what you are afraid to do.* In hope we live—in despair we die. The coward dies a hundred deaths—the brave but one.

> " Each hour the trembling coward dies—
> 'Tis courage only lives."

Courage is not born in us, but is often the result of training and discipline; we ought, it has been said, every day to conquer a fear, and, above all, the fear of death. An unwearied spiritual energy which absorbs the idea of death in the glowing consciousness of life, is one of the signs of a healthy, vigorous soul, for—

> " Whatever crazy sorrow saith,
> No life that breathes with human breath
> Hath ever truly wished for death.
> 'Tis life of which our nerves are scant ;
> O life, not death, for which we pant,
> More life and fuller that we want."

It is only the coward who says, "My life, my life, everything for my life," for he is generally a shuffler, a timeserver, one who would turn and turn again, and do anything

---

* Emerson.

mean and despicable to save that miserable skin of his. He is constantly fidgeting and repeating some worldly-wise maxim of the copybook order of morality. He can understand his ledger better than he can his bible, and his chief concerns in life are to save a little money and to save his little soul. In his eyes the "Book of Martyrs" must be a book of madmen, for he would not have given his penny where the martyr gave his soul. If he is in a position of honour and trust he is fertile in evasions, and, like Swift's courtier, he never refuses or keeps a promise. He is full of trepidations, and in danger would consider absence of body better than presence of mind. You can only know of the existence of his soul by its paroxysms, as the invalid the existence of his stomach by its qualms. He is, after all, but the miserable caricature of a man.

But let us turn his picture to the wall, and look upon the form and front of a brave man, who, unlike the coward or sneak, is to be known by what he is, for his character is positive. If good, he has the courage of virtue; if bad, though he may make vice detestable, yet he does not make it contemptible. He may be a soldier of God or of the devil, in either case he is a soldier; and whether his forces are moral, spiritual, or physical, he has courage, valour, and the greatness of action, which includes immoral as well as moral greatness. The great success of Luther was due to his indomitable will. Trusting in God, he defied the pope and the devil, and that at a time when the pope was the sovereign of Christendom, and supposed to be gifted with supernatural powers, and the devil was not regarded as a myth. When he was warned not to go to the Diet of Worms because foul play was intended, and he would be murdered if he went, he exclaimed, "Go to Worms! I will go if there are as many devils in Worms as there are tiles upon the roofs of the houses." Everything serves a brave soul and does homage to it. It was said of one, an admiral, "It seemed as if the sea stood in awe of him." Courage will provoke even its enemies to admiration. When James II. witnessed from the steeple of La Hogue the reckless intrepidity of the sailors under Admiral Russell, he cried out, " My brave English! My brave English!" forgetting entirely that they were fighting against himself, and completing the ruin of his own cause. Napoleon could testify his admiration for the obstinate courage of the British soldiers, who never knew when they were beaten. Demosthenes has given us an example of the courage of the soldier. Speaking of Philip of Macedon he says, "I saw him, though covered with wounds, his eye struck out, his collar bone broke, maimed both in his hands and feet, still resolutely rush into the midst of dangers, and ready to deliver up to Fortune any part of his body she might desire, provided he might live honourably and gloriously with the rest." The true martyr defies the rack, the fire, and the hangman. He tells the tyrant that he has the power to die and to scorn him, for he can say—

> "The visage of the hangman frights not me;
> The sight of whips, racks, gibbets, axes, fires,
> Are scaffoldings on which my soul climbs up
> To an eternal habitation."

The courage which springs from love and affection is of the greatest. The tales of chivalry are all founded on the sentiment of love, honour, and devotion. There is one place where even the coward becomes brave—in defence of his home. One of the most pathetic stories ever told of the devotion of love and persistency of will, which savours the highest heroism, is that chronicled by John of Brompton, of the mother of Thomas-à-Becket. His father, Gilbert-à-Becket, was taken prisoner during one of the crusades, by a Syrian Emir, and detained for a considerable time in honourable captivity. A daughter of the Emir saw him at her father's table, heard him converse, fell in love with him, and offered to arrange the means by which both might escape to Europe. The project only partly succeeded: he escaped, but she was left behind. Soon afterwards, however, she contrived to elude her attendants, and after many marvellous adventures by sea and land, arrived in England, knowing but two English words, "London" and "Gilbert." By constantly repeating the first, she was directed to the city, and there followed by a mob. She walked for months, from street to street, crying as she went, "Gilbert! Gilbert!" She at last came to the street in which her lover lived. The mob and the name attracted the attention of a servant in the house; Gilbert recognized her, and they were married.

It will be noted that in all men born to rule, whatever qualities they may lack, there is always the firm adamantine will. It is really the will that makes the character, and "character," says Novalis, "is destiny." He who wavers, halts between two opinions, and is always undecided, whatever his gifts may be, will never be a great, and very rarely a good man. It is to show what this willpower can do that we shall give an example of the soldier, the patriot, the statesman, and make a few remarks upon religious heroism.

There are lives which stamp their influence upon their age and upon all time by stern, resolute action. Such were the lives of Cæsar, Alexander, and Napoleon; men who made the earth tremble beneath their feet, who found even this world too small a theatre to play their parts in—

> "Whose game was empire, and whose stakes were thrones,
> Whose table earth, whose dice were human bones."

Such men seem to possess a magnetic power over all those brought within the sphere of their personal attraction. They have that "mystery of commanding, of winning, fettering, wielding, moulding, banding the hearts of millions till they move as one." Before such men no Alpine difficulty can obstruct or hinder; they dare impossibilities, and force themselves onward " along the line of limitless desires," breaking down all barriers, and making every path straight before them.

> "Their life is like a battle, and a march,
> And like a wind blast, never resting, homeless
> They storm across the war-convulsed earth."

Well might an old writer say "that the heart of man is a small matter: it is not enough for a kite's dinner, yet the whole world will not contain it."

Take Cæsar's life, for instance, as an example of strength of will and audacity of mind. His was an unrelenting yet flexible will of etherial strength, not like the ordinary iron will of the conqueror. Keen, subtle, quick sighted, his powers vital in every part, were capable of intense and instantaneous concentration. His hands were immediately connected with his head; for his thoughts were actions, and his language events. His life reads like an epic poem, a poem dedicated to his own deity—the deity of self. Before he had reached his twentieth year he had the hardihood to engage in a struggle with the Dictator Sylla, and flying from his wrath, he fell into the hands of pirates; even these cruel and inhuman wretches were awed and subdued by his presence, and when they fixed his ransom at 20 talents, "It is too little," he said, "you shall have 50; but, once free, I will crucify everyone of you!"—and he kept his word. His extraordinary presence of mind discovered means of safety amid sudden reverses; even on the brink of ruin he was always himself, and could turn the worst omens to his own advantage. He stumbled once in going ashore to take possession of a province. In an instant he turned the attention of his followers, who would have augured ill of his success, by exclaiming, "Thus, and by this contact with the earth, do I take possession of thee, O Africa!" The whole history of his campaign against the Gauls is one of daring impossibilities. In these wars, in somewhat less than 10 years, he took by storm above 800 cities, and subdued 300 nations, and fought with three millions of men at different times, of which he destroyed one million in battle, and took as many prisoners. He could break men in like dogs; when his favourite legions mutinied, he abandoned them before they could desert him, and made them crouch at his feet for forgiveness. In Spain, his soldiers, disheartened and dismayed, would not obey his order to attack the vast numbers opposed to them; seizing a shield, he exclaimed, "I will die here!" and rushed singly upon the enemy's ranks; a shower of arrows flew against him, when within a few paces of the enemy his soldiers rallied and charged for his support. The majority of his soldiers, when they fell into the enemy's hands, refused to accept their lives on the condition of serving against him.

At Rome, when he heard of plots to assassinate him, he dismissed his guards and walked about unarmed and alone, for he said "that it was better to die, than to be always expecting death." Well might his "honourable assassins" when their bloody work was done, wonder that so small and shrivelled a body could have contained so large a soul. But Cæsar by his daring dared too much. He defied the laws of the republic, and justly forfeited his life according to the laws of the state. Cæsar was the representative of the Roman mind, of its strength and weakness, its glory and degradation; everything he planned and carried out was on a colossal scale; he bribed as no monarch has ever bribed before or since. He flattered the multitude by a series of magnificent displays, such as the world had never before witnessed, in honour of his triumphs and victories.

He represented also the utilitarian practical spirit of the Roman people (a people who know nothing of metaphysics or of abstract philosophy). He made roads, built bridges, and when struck down in the meridian of his glory, was only beginning to carry out a series of gigantic achievements. No wonder that after his death his countrymen deified him, for men make gods after their own image. We think it is from this apotheosis of Cæsar may be traced the first signs of the degeneration of the Roman nation. Cæsar failed; as every selfish and unworthy aim fails. Though he conquered the whole world he could not rule the "empire of himself." What Emerson says of

Napoleon is true of him also. "It was not his fault, he did all that in him lay to live and thrive without moral principle. It was the nature of things, the eternal law of man, and of the world which baulked and ruined him; and the result in a million of experiments will be the same. Every experiment by multitudes or by individuals that has a sensual and selfish aim will fail." Cæsar failed, and his dynasty failed also, for it was founded on force and rested not on any moral foundation.

The patriot who puts aside personal ambition, and struggles for the defence of his country, must ever hold a higher rank than he who fights, however bravely, for his own aggrandisement and glory. It is well for our own country that it has never, when occasion required, wanted such men as the former.

We take William the Silent, Prince of Orange, the hero of the Dutch Republic, as a worthy representative of disinterested patriotism. His life and deeds have been well written by Mr. Motley in his "History of the Rise of the Dutch Republic." Though the Prince of Orange was but the sovereign of a small and insignificant principality, yet he successfully resisted the mightiest monarch of the world, Philip the Second of Spain. At the onset of his career he was a Roman Catholic, yet his soul sickened at the horrible cruelties he saw perpetrated in the holy name of religion, and when as a hostage in France he discovered, through the French king, the intention of Philip to plant the inquisition in the Netherlands, and to extirpate Protestantism, he never faltered one moment in his determination to resist that iniquitous scheme. He felt, to use his own words, "that an Inquisition for the Netherlands had been resolved upon more cruel than that of Spain, since it would need but to look askance at an image to be cast into the flames, and he could not but feel compassion for so many virtuous men and women thus devoted to massacre." While silently waiting and watching the course of events his mind underwent a change; he renounced Catholicism, and joined what were then called "the accursed vermin," the Protestants. Thenceforth he became a soldier of the Reformation, and with firm faith he committed to God his cause and trust. "I have resolved," he said, in one of his letters, "to place myself in the hands of the Almighty, that he may guide me whither it is His good pleasure that I should go. I see well enough that I am destined to pass this life in misery and labour, with which I am well content since it thus pleases the Omnipotent, for I know that I have merited still greater chastisement. I only implore Him graciously to send me strength to endure with patience."

Brave words for a rich and noble prince, who preferred a life of misery and labour doing his duty, to one of ease, comfort, and worldly honour. What he prayed for was what all noble souls pray for—strength. With a small and undisciplined army he resisted host after host of the finest armies of Spain, commanded by the best captains of the age, fighting sometimes by sea, sometimes by land, sometimes in the bowels of the earth, or breast high in water; sometimes within blazing cities, or upon fields of ice on skates; in one extremity piercing the dykes and letting loose the sea upon their enemies, for these Hollanders in the heroism of their despair said, "Better a drowned land than a lost land."

The Netherlands were made the cockpit of Europe, and no crime is there to be found in ancient or modern history to be compared to that hellish edict whereby all the inhabitants of the Netherlands were condemned to death as heretics. Under this edict more than fifty thousand human beings were deliberately murdered. Their cities were given up to pillage, and the worst crimes were committed by the cruelest of all soldiers; their country was turned into a desert, and consumed as by a prairie fire. Their murderers went to work with the priests' baptism on their swords, and were rewarded by the prayers and benisons of the clergy. Oh, religion! what crimes have been committed in thy name! The most cruel deeds ever perpetrated on this fair earth have been done in the name of conscience, when men have killed each other from a sense of right and duty. Sometimes by quarrelling over and torturing one poor word out of all sense and meaning, like dogs snarling, growling, and fighting over a bone without any flesh upon it, for there can be no better subject for a religious dispute than when there is not a particle of evidence to prove one side or the other. "Ten thousand people," says Sydney Smith, "have been burnt before now, or hanged, for one proposition. The proposition had no meaning. Looked into and examined in these days it is absolute nonsense." Ought not the lessons of the past to teach us toleration, or, in the words of Coleridge, to be "tolerant of everything except intolerance?" When Philip found he could not conquer the forces of William, in a frenzy of cowardice at the loss of his dominions he tried bribes. There was nothing he could desire for himself and his family that would not be granted—millions of money, estates, titles, but the Prince of Orange repelled these advances made to him with scorn. "Neither for property," he said, "nor for life, neither for wife, nor for children, would he mix in his cup a single drop of treason."

When all these things failed, a ban was issued against him, and a price set upon his head; the assassin, however vile and criminal, was promised the highest honours of the state, and to be ennobled. This edict perhaps surpasses any other for its sanctified imprecation. Unless Christ can be allied with Belial—truth with falsehood, and justice with cruelty—then, and only then, could this hellish edict be justified! Against this ban William wrote and issued his famous apology, which must have made his cowering enemies wince; they were the words of a man living man-like, addressed to men who were living and acting devil-like; who did not believe in the force of argument, but only in the rack, the fire, and the sword. Some extracts from this apology will better show his character than could otherwise be presented. Repelling with scorn the project of assassination, he said :—" I am in the hands of God, my worldly goods and my life have been long since dedicated to His service. He will dispose of them as seems best for His glory and my salvation." In conclusion he addressed his countrymen in these words:—
" Would to God that my perpetual banishment, or even my death, could bring you a true deliverance from so many calamities! Oh, how consoling would be such banishment—how sweet such a death! For why have I exposed my property? Was it that I might enrich myself? Why have I lost my brothers? Was it that I might find new

ones? Why have I left my son so long a prisoner? Can you give me another? Why have I put my life so often in danger? What reward can I hope after my long services, and the almost total wreck of my earthly fortunes, if not the prize of having acquired, perhaps at the expense of my life, your liberty? If then, my masters, you judge that my absence or my death can serve you, behold me ready to obey. Command me—send me to the ends of the earth—I will obey! Here is my head, over which no prince, no monarch has power but yourselves. Dispose of it for your good, for the preservation of your republic; but if you judge that the moderate amount of experience and industry which is in me, if you judge that the remainder of my property and of my life can yet be of service to you, I dedicate them afresh to you and to the country."

But the issue of the ban soon began to have an effect; assassin after assassin was sent from Spain; within two years there had been five attempts to murder the prince, a sixth, which was successful, was soon to follow—and William, Prince of Orange, the Saviour of his country, was struck down by the hand of a paid assassin of the most holy and catholic king!

To the end he stood firm and resolute, trusting in God, neither elated by success nor depressed by defeat, "caring nothing for threats or menaces in any matter when he could act with a clear conscience, and without doing injury to his neighbour;" calmly smiling in the greatest extremity of danger, for he had faced death too often to be afraid of it. He lived not for himself, but for his country, and his dying words were " O, my God! have mercy upon this poor people." "As long as he lived," says Motley' "he was the guiding star of a whole brave nation; and when he died the little children cried in the streets."

In concluding these remarks upon William, Prince of Orange, we might say that he was one of those great, *silent* men. Let this be noted, he knew how to be silent when others would have spoken. It has been well said that he who knows not how to hold his tongue knows not how to talk. This faculty of keeping silence is one of the rarest, especially in these days of liberty of speech, when to say and do as one likes is the ideal of liberty. In this strange Babel-like confusion of much talking, when to say something is thought to be the same as something to say, may not the tongue be well compared to a racehorse, the least weight it carries the faster it goes?

In these days of telegrams, unlicensed press, newspaper correspondents, and stump orators, the figure of William the Silent stands unique. As he stood face to face with the French king, and heard the design of Philip to plant the Inquisition in the Netherlands, he remained silent, for which he received the name, and his silence gained him the victory. Had he spoken, and there had been telegrams flashing the news abroad, special correspondents writing home, and stump orators denouncing the tyranny of the act, William the Silent might have lived in vain.

As a type of the patriotic statesman, we have selected one of our own countrymen, William Pitt, Earl of Chatham. At his advent England was steeped in corruption. Bribery was the great ruling power; to bribe well was to govern, for each man, according to Walpole, had his price. Except in Charles II.'s time our nation had never before sunk so low in corruption and degradation. Her armies had been defeated; her navy nearly destroyed. Such were our disasters by sea and by land that the imperturbable Earl Chesterfield said in despair, "We are no longer a nation."

Her social position was no better. If there was nothing but corruption in high places, drunkenness and brutality reigned below, and lawlessness was law. "Gin," says a modern author, "had been discovered in 1684, and about half a century later England consumed seven millions of gallons. The tavern-keepers on their sign-boards invited people to come and get drunk for a penny; for twopence they might get dead drunk; no charge for straw. The landlord dragged those who succumbed into a cellar, where they slept off their carouse. You could not walk London streets without meeting wretches incapable of motion or thought, lying in the kennel, whom the care of the passers by alone could prevent from being smothered in mud or crushed by carriage-wheels." Mob law reigned supreme when a tax was imposed to stop this madness; the act could not be carried into execution without an armed force, and ultimately it was withdrawn. "England had been a long time in labour," said Frederick the Great of Prussia, "but she at length brought forth a man; that man was William Pitt," and we might say that of men who are born kings Pitt was one. He was the only man who was conscious of his own powers and had faith in the resources of the nation, "I know that I can save the country" said he, "and I know no other man can." This was no idle vaunt. He did save his country, and raised it to the highest pinnacle of greatness; during his administration he reigned. He infused his own spirit into everything, and every one around him was inspired by his presence. Every one felt the soul of Chatham glowing in his own breast, and so exerted himself to the utmost of his ability. "No man" said a soldier of the time, "ever entered Pitt's closet who did not feel himself braver when he came out than when he went in." The whole continent of Europe, India, and America soon felt the influence of his powerful will on the nation.

"Man alone," says Emerson, "can perform the Impossible." Chatham, like Napoleon, defied impossibilities. When Lord Anson at the Admiralty sent word to him that it was impossible to carry out his orders in time, Chatham was confined to his chamber with a violent attack of gout. "Impossible!" says Chatham, turning upon the messenger an eye glaring like the furnace of the Cyclops, "who talks to me of impossibilities?" Starting up and conquering his agony for a moment, he stamped his foot upon the floor, and exclaimed, "Tell Lord Anson that he serves under a minister who treads on impossibilities." Chatham was one of those true patriots who, though they love their country well, love mankind more. He did not believe in that sentiment, not unfrequently quoted, "Our country right or wrong." During the American struggle for independence, he protested against that iniquitous war, for he viewed the Americans as English subjects, struggling for English legal rights and privileges, and would never regard them as rebels. When driven from office, broken down and shattered in health, he told the nation "You cannot conquer America," yet he retained to the last the idea that she might be conciliated and united to the mother country in federal union, as our colonies are at present. Such a chance of union might have occurred had he lived, but his death dissipated all such hopes.

But, says the small critic whose business is to chronicle the failings of men, Chatham had great faults. Yes, we answer, all great men have great faults, and he is a poor critic who can see only these faults, " Who seeks for goodness should himself be good."* It is only in one Being that we can honour perfect human nature. "The greatest of all faults," says Carlyle, " is to be conscious of none." Shakespeare says truly:—

> "They say best men are moulded out of faults,
> And for the most become much more the better
> For being a little bad."

It is our duty to strive after perfection, though we never can attain it, for a "perfect monster" is a perfect lie. Chatham was great with all his imperfections, and not in spite of them; he who hates a man because of his errors and failings must hate all mankind, and if this same stern censor's faults were written upon his forehead, he would pull his hat over his eyes, or all his life, like Parson Hooper,† wear a black veil.

Religious heroism is higher and deeper, nobler and purer, than any other. To die in the cause and for the love of truth is more worthy than to shed one's blood for the love of glory or for country; but better than dying is that of living in the service and for the love of truth. The highest life of man must ever be the religious life, which only can fully develop the rich and manifold energies of the soul, and raise it above the dust and din of wordly strife,

---

* Goethe.   † Hawthorne's "Twice told Tales.'

above the clouds of self and passion into the higher region of a divine communion.

> "Unless above himself he can
> Erect himself, how poor a thing is man."

Tear, cripple, crush and maim the soul as you may by crime or by error, it will still in times of distress turn and look up to heaven. The true Christian life is an heroic one. It may be a quiet life with nameless deeds, but the world is richer and better for all time because of its diffusive influence. "The growing good of the world," says a modern author, "is partly dependent on unhistoric acts; and that things are not so ill with you and me, as they might have been, is half owing to the number who lived faithfully a hidden life, and rest in unvisited tombs."

Perhaps in this 19th century it is more difficult to live an heroic life than in any preceding one; as christianity develops, the higher will be the christian ideal. "Be ye perfect, even as your Father which is in heaven is perfect." Our religion teaches us self-denial, submission, and resignation—the hardest lessons of life. It requires more courage to be silent under provocation than to strike, more strength to subdue passion than to give way to it, to forgive instead of revenge, to overcome evil with good, and sometimes more courage to live than to die. In our prosperity we are surrounded by temptations and dangers We think we are strong when we are weak, and weak when we are strong. "How many men," says Carlyle, "can stand adversity who cannot bear prosperity." So with nations. In times of danger we often feel God near us, when in prosperity we do not feel his need. "In the perplexities of nations," says Ruskin, "in their struggles

for existence, in their infancy, their impotence, or even
their disorganization, they have higher hopes and nobler
passions. Out of the suffering comes the serious mind;
out of the salvation the grateful heart; out of endurance,
fortitude; out of deliverance, faith; but when they have
learned to live under providence of laws, and with decency
and justice of regard for each other, and when they have
done away with violent and external sources of suffering,
worse evils seem to arise out of their rest, evils that vex
less and mortify more, that suck the blood though they do
not shed it, and ossify the heart though they do not torture
it. And deep though the causes of thankfulness must be
to every people at peace with others and at unity in itself,
there are causes of fear, also, a fear greater than of sword
and sedition; that dependence on God may be forgotten,
because the bread is given and the water sure; that
gratitude to Him may cease, because His constancy of protection has taken the semblance of a natural law, that
heavenly hope may grow faint amidst the full fruition of
the world; that selfishness may take place of undemanded
devotion, compassion be lost in vain glory, and love in
dissimulation; that enervation may succeed to strength,
apathy to patience; and the noise of jesting words and
foulness of dark thoughts, to the earnest purity of the
girded loins and the burning lamp. Above the river of human
life there is a wintry wind, though a heavenly sunshine;
the iris colours its agitation, the frost fixes upon its repose.
Let us beware that our rest become not the rest of stones,
which so long as they are torrent-tossed and thunder-
stricken, maintain their majesty; but when the stream is
silent, and the storm passed, suffer the grass to cover

them, and the lichen to feed on them, and are ploughed down into dust." But hopefully let us look upon our much-abused nineteenth century. It has its good signs even in these so-called evil times. (The golden age is always before and behind us). It has its spiritual heroes, who are doing work bravely against the empire of darkness and wrong, not for personal triumph, but for the glory of God and the advance of His kingdom; some in the benighted corners of the earth, the abode of superstition, cruelty, and lust; others in our sin-stricken cities, battling with those evil spirits, the demoniacal vices and passions of men; some perishing in the eternal snows of the north; others, like Livingstone, under the burning zone of Africa, yielding up their breath with joy—"a joy," says an old writer, "which will put on a more glorious garment above, and be a joy superinvested in glory!" It is generally thought that in the shop and market-place religious heroism is rather at a low ebb. Cicero, in his time, spoke of trade as absolutely base, mean, and dishonourable; certainly we have advanced beyond that state. In trade and commerce there are a thousand temptations which beset men at every step where competition is keen and men are not over scrupulous in their dealings one with another. Honour to him who would sacrifice a bargain rather than sell his soul, because he knows that if he swindles his neighbour he swindles himself more than he does his victim; he is far better than he who has a more tender conscience about his *opinions* than he has about his *actions*, and whose conscientious opinions, whatever they may be, in these days of universal toleration, cost him nothing.

If Hell is paved with good intentions, it is probably, with good opinions also; but we may be sure that Heaven is full of good works. According to one of the mystics, "God is only an eternal will to all goodness." "The life of religion," says Swedenborg, "is to do good." There must be a spontaneity of action as well as a spontaneity of thought and feeling. A man *must* live according to his faith, and whatever opinions or doctrines he may profess, they are worthless if his daily life give the lie to them. It is only the church of Rome who holds that "a lazy, ragged, filthy saint, not over scrupulous of truth," is preferable to a "just, upright, generous, honourable, and conscientious" sinner,* and that a mystic rite of supernatural power shall at the last moment make that "lazy, filthy, lying saint" a fit inheritor of the kingdom of heaven.

There is a story told that Athanasius was once asked his opinion on the common practice of death-bed baptisms. He replied with an apologue which admitted of no rejoinder, "An angel once said to my great predecessor Peter (the bishop of the see before Alexander), Why do you send me these sacks (these wind-bags) carefully sealed up with nothing whatever inside?" †

Let not our souls be mere wind-bags, but let them be filled with good and noble thoughts which will form their character, and fit them for good and noble deeds.

We have attempted in a very imperfect manner to pourtray the heroic spirit as it animates the soldier, the patriot, the statesman, and the saint. True heroism is the highest

---

* John Henry Newman.
† Dean Stanley's Lectures on the History of the Eastern Church.

expression of the unconquerable spirit in man. It inspires the noble soul with an enthusiasm for humanity and believes in its eternal progressive life. According to the theory of evolution "The whole constitution of our minds has been formed by experience, not by our own only, but by the accumulated experience of all our ancestors handed down by hereditary transmission."† If so, the evolution of humanity has been contemporaneous with the evolution of mind, and we believe that humanity alone through successive generations, continuous in intellect, and by the various contributions of the forces and faculties of its members, is capable of gradually evolving and perfecting the will of God on earth. And we may be sure that if we lose faith in humanity it is the negation of progress.

We recognise the heroic spirit, not only in those deeds which embellish history with all the splendours of romance, but also in that lowly life, loyal to duty, whose actions no history will record, no poetry celebrate, and of whose praises the word will be mute. This spirit animates the poet, as it did Milton, with the highest ambition. "To celebrate in glorious and lofty hymns the throne and equipage of God's almightiness, and what He suffers to be wrought with high providence in His church; to sing victorious agonies of martyrs and saints, the deeds and triumphs of just and pious nations, doing valiantly through faith against the enemies of Christ; to deplore the general relapses of kingdoms and states from justice and God's true worship."

In conclusion, we shall quote a hymn of the German

---

* Herbert Spencer.

poet, Richter, which well describes the character of the Christian hero.

"The Christian life, how bright within it glows;
 Although the sun may bronze the wanderer's brow,
The precious treasure heaven's high King bestows,
 None but themselves can recognise or know.
  What though no eye hath scann'd,
   Untouch'd by mortal hand,
Yet on their heart its beams of beauty shine;
It clothes them with a dignity divine.

"They to the outward eye but wretched are,—
 To angels seem neglected and abhorr'd;
Yet inwardly are brides of beauty rare,—
 The coronal, the pleasure of the Lord.
  The marvel of all time,
   Soaring from earth's cold clime
T' embrace the King in robes of sunny light,
Who feeds His sheep among the lilies white.

"They tread the earth, but ah! they live in heaven;
 Seem powerless, yet the world protect and bless;
In danger's midst their hearts are still unriven,
 Poorest, yet all things needful they possess.
  Though troubles oft annoy,
   Yet are they fill'd with joy;
Though to the outward eye the slaves of death,
Yet inwardly they live the life of faith.

* * * * *

"Jesus! Thou hidden life-blood of the heart,
 Mysterious Monarch of the world unseen,
Help us to choose the good, the better part,
 Though men with Thy black cross reproach us keen.
  Branded with evil name,
   Sons of rebuke and shame,
Here living with the Lord unseen, unknown,
Oh, that in heaven we may surround His throne."